MACHINE LEARNING INTERVIEW QUESTIONS

VEENA A AND GOWRISHANKAR S

Chennai • Bangalore

CLEVER FOX PUBLISHING
Chennai, India

Published by CLEVER FOX PUBLISHING 2024
Copyright © Veena A and Gowrishankar S 2024

All Rights Reserved.
ISBN: 978-93-56488-39-7

This book has been published with all reasonable efforts taken to make the material error-free after the consent of the author. No part of this book shall be used, reproduced in any manner whatsoever without written permission from the author, except in the case of brief quotations embodied in critical articles and reviews.

The Author of this book is solely responsible and liable for its content including but not limited to the views, representations, descriptions, statements, information, opinions and references ["Content"]. The Content of this book shall not constitute or be construed or deemed to reflect the opinion or expression of the Publisher or Editor. Neither the Publisher nor Editor endorse or approve the Content of this book or guarantee the reliability, accuracy or completeness of the Content published herein and do not make any representations or warranties of any kind, express or implied, including but not limited to the implied warranties of merchantability, fitness for a particular purpose. The Publisher and Editor shall not be liable whatsoever for any errors, omissions, whether such errors or omissions result from negligence, accident, or any other cause or claims for loss or damages of any kind, including without limitation, indirect or consequential loss or damage arising out of use, inability to use, or about the reliability, accuracy or sufficiency of the information contained in this book.

I would love to dedicate this book to my parents, and my family for their love, support and encouragement.

– Dr. Veena A

To my dad, Dr. S. Surendranath for his unconditional love and unwavering faith in me.

– Dr. Gowrishankar S.

CONTENTS

Preface .... *v*
Acknowledgment .... *ix*
Authors .... *xi*

1. Introduction 1
2. Statistics 10
3. Probability and Hypothesis 51
4. Gradient Descent 72
5. Introduction to Machine Learning 78
6. K- Nearest Neighbors 100
7. Naïve Bayes 110
8. Regression 114
9. Decision Trees 130
10. Neural Networks 148
11. Deep Learning 162

Bibliography *201*
Index *202*
About the front cover page design *208*

PREFACE

Students will find that the ideas of machine learning are presented in this book in a way that is easy to understand. The objective of this book is to test the candidate's understanding of the subject through a series of questions. These questions should cover topics such as supervised and unsupervised learning, neural networks, decision trees, gradient descent, and other related topics. A good candidate should also be able to explain algorithms and their applications, as well as discuss the pros and cons of various machine learning techniques. Ultimately, these questions should reveal the candidate's level of knowledge and ability to think critically about the subject.

This book of machine learning interview questions differs from other technical interviews in that they focus more on understanding the theoretical aspects of the subject than on the technical details. The questions are designed to assess a candidate's understanding of the underlying principles of machine learning and their ability to apply them to real-world problems. This type of interview also allows the interviewer to probe deeper into the candidate's understanding of the subject and their ability to think critically about the topic.

The prerequisites for machine learning vary depending on the type of machine learning to be done. Generally, it is recommended that candidates have a good understanding of mathematics and statistics, as understanding these topics is essential for working with machine learning algorithms. A basic knowledge of programming is also helpful, as most machine learning algorithms are written in code and it is easier to understand the concepts. Additionally, some understanding of linear algebra, calculus, and probability theory will help when working with more advanced machine learning algorithms.

This book can be used by students to assess their knowledge, understanding, and skills. Questions may focus on the student's reasons for pursuing the Machine Learning domain, their experience with research in machine learning, and their ability to think critically and solve problems. Also, questions can range from general questions about a student's background to specific questions about their academic goals and achievements. This type of interview can be used to assess whether a student is a good fit for an machine learning program.

This book provides a comprehensive guide to understanding the core ideas behind Machine Learning. We have high hopes that students who read this book will walk away with an understanding of the wonder, brilliance, and immense value of machine learning, and we also hope that they will have fun while learning.

Organization of Chapters

Here's a brief rundown of what you will find in each chapter:

In Chapter 1 of the book, the distinction between data science and data analytics, as well as the many forms of analytics, are discussed. Additionally, mentioned are the various data types, as well as the variables that are used in data analytics.

The definitions of statistics, probability, and distributions are all discussed in detail in Chapter 2 of the book. The techniques for sampling the population, skewness and the several forms it takes, and the hypothesis are all described here.

In Chapter 3, the two related concepts probability and hypothesis are explained. The many modes of distribution, along with some instances of each, are dissected here. The various methods of hypothesis testing, as well as their benefits and drawbacks, are also covered in this chapter.

In Chapter 4, gradient descent, an optimization algorithm that is commonly used to train machine learning models is explained along with its types and definitions for terminologies like step function, global and local minima, and learning rate.

Chapter 5 discusses the types of machine learning algorithms. It also lists the differences between supervised and unsupervised algorithms. Moreover, terms like classification, regression overfitting, bias, and variance are expressed in this section.

Chapter 6 and Chapter 7, explains the working of K-NN and Naïve Bayes' algorithm, respectively.

Topics such as regression, types of regression, L1 and L2 regularization are explained in Chapter 8.

Creation of decision trees, information gain and entropy are covered in Chapter 9.

Chapter 10 and Chapter 11, describes neural networks and deep learning concepts.

Who Should Read This Book?

This book is geared towards those with little to moderate experience who are interested in learning about machine learning or preparing for an interview in the machine learning domain.

Support for the Book

We will try to address your questions within an appropriate timeframe. Understand that we have a day job just like you and we may not be able to respond immediately. Rest assured, we will respond to genuine questions and we do not like to keep our readers in the dark whatsoever.

This Book Is Not for You

If you are expecting to implement different Machine Learning models using Python programming language, then this book is not for you. The questions are not tailored to the specific needs of a single company or an organization.

Errata

We hope to improve this book continually. If you have any suggestions for improving this text or if an error should be found, the authors would be grateful if the notifications were sent by email to gowrishankarnath@acm.org. To ensure your messages do not end up in our junk mail folder, please include the subject as "Machine Learning Interview Questions".

ACKNOWLEDGMENT

As a fun and creative exercise, "Machine Learning Interview Questions" is a must-have resource. Making this book a reality takes many dedicated people and it is my great pleasure to acknowledge their contributions. I am grateful to Dr. Gowrishankar S., who first conceived the idea of writing this book and kept faith in me, and gave me an opportunity to be the co-author of this book. I wish to acknowledge the direct and indirect contributions and assistance of various colleagues and friends with whom I have collaborated. Reviewers play a very important role in the development of the manuscript. My heartfelt thanks to Dr. Srinivasa A. H., Associate Professor, Dept. of CSE, Dr. AIT, Bengaluru, Karnataka, India and Dr. Thara D. K., Professor and HEAD, Dept. of ISE, CIT, Gubbi, Karnataka, India for reviewing the contents of the book. My husband and daughter kept me on my toes during the writing of this book and I'm indebted to them for their time and patience. I would like to thank our publisher, Clever Fox Publishing, and their team for the excellent collaboration, follow-up and timely replies to emails. I count on our readers to enjoy our book and welcome any suggestions and feedback for the improvement of this book.

Dr. Veena A.

The primary goal of this book is to make the interview process for the machine learning domain as painless as possible.

Acknowledgment

Writing a book is never easy and is quite challenging. It took a lot of effort on our part to get "Machine Learning Interview Questions" to its meaningful conclusion. My co-author, Dr. Veena A., has strived hard to present the complex technical information about the machine learning domain to be as accessible as possible for the readers of this book. I appreciate her for stimulating great ideas while writing this book.

And last, but most importantly, I have no words to express my gratitude to my family for their motivation and for going out of their way to support me during tiring times.

We hope the reader enjoys reading this book as much as we enjoyed writing it.

Dr. Gowrishankar S.

AUTHORS

$\mathcal{D}$r. Veena A. is currently working as an Assistant Professor in the Department of Computer Science and Engineering at Dr. Ambedkar Institute of Technology, Bengaluru, India. She earned her Ph.D. in Computer Science and Engineering, M.Tech., in Computer Science and Engineering and B.E. in Information Science and Engineering from Visvesvaraya Technological University (VTU), Belagavi, India.

She has worked as a Member Technical Staff at C-DAC and as a software developer at Envision Network Technologies Pvt. Ltd.

She has published papers in various reputable international journals and conferences. She has delivered many keynote addresses and invited talks on machine learning and deep learning. She has co-authored a book and has earned five granted patents. Her research interests include automated machine learning, deep learning, image processing, natural language processing, and reinforcement learning in the smart healthcare domain.

Dr. Gowrishankar S. is currently working as a Professor in the Department of Computer Science and Engineering at Dr. Ambedkar Institute of Technology, Bengaluru, Karnataka, Bharat.

He earned his M.B.A. in Marketing Management from Indira Gandhi National Open University (IGNOU), New Delhi, Bharat in 2020, Ph.D. in Engineering from the Faculty of Engineering and Technology, Jadavpur University, Kolkata, Bharat in 2010, M.Tech. in Software Engineering from Visvesvaraya Technological University (VTU), Belagavi, Bharat in 2005 and B.E. in Computer Science and Engineering from Visvesvaraya Technological University (VTU), Belagavi, Bharat, in 2003.

From 2011 to 2014, he worked as Senior Research Scientist and Tech Lead at Honeywell Technology Solutions, Bengaluru, Bharat. He was awarded the Technical and Innovation Award and Individual Excellence Award for his contribution to the successful delivery of projects at Honeywell Technology Solutions.

He has published several papers in various reputed International Journals and Conferences. He is serving as editor and reviewer for various prestigious International Journals. He has delivered many keynote addresses and invited talks throughout Bharat on a variety of topics related to Computer Science and Engineering. He was instrumental in organizing several conferences, webinars, workshops, and seminars. He has served on the panel of several Academic Bodies of Universities and Autonomous Colleges as a BOS and BOE member. He has co-authored a book and has earned six granted patents. He regularly carries out consultancy services for other organizations.

His current research efforts are mainly focused on the applications and implications of Machine Learning, Deep Learning and Data Analytics for the upliftment of society.

CHAPTER 1

INTRODUCTION

1. Define Data

ANSWER   Data refers to the information collected or observed from a particular source, such as experiments, surveys, observations, or measurements. This data can take various forms, including numerical, categorical, or ordinal, and it serves as the foundation for statistical analysis and inference. Some examples of data are the temperature of the city, stock related data, height, length, size, weight, and so on.

2. Define Variable and the types of data used in Machine Learning and Statistics.

ANSWER   A variable is a characteristic of each individual element of population or sample. In statistics, we distinguish between two distinct categories of data as shown in the figure 1.1.
1. Qualitative Data Type / Categorical Data
    a. Nominal Data
    b. Ordinal Data
2. Quantitative Data Type / Numerical Data
    a. Discrete Data
    b. Continuous Data

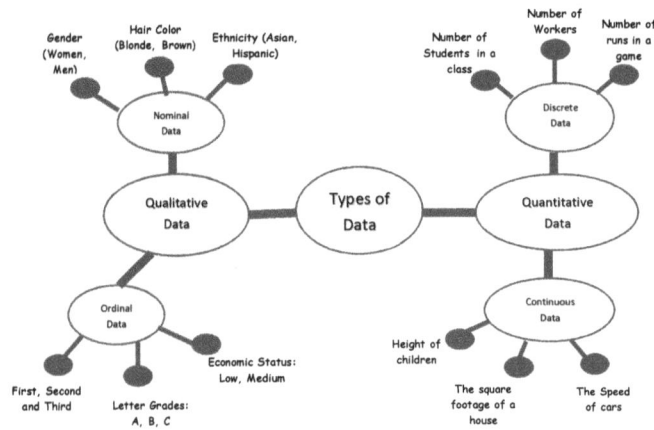

Figure 1.1: Types of Data in Machine Learning and Statistics

3. **Explain the Qualitative and Quantitative Data Types.**

ANSWER Qualitative or categorical data refers to data that cannot be measured numerically but instead relies on qualities, characteristics, or attributes. This type of data is descriptive and is often subjective in nature. Examples of qualitative data include colors, emotions, opinions, and preferences.

Qualitative data analysis includes techniques, such as content analysis, which identifies themes and patterns in the data, and discourse analysis, which examines language and communication. Qualitative data can also be visualized using data visualization techniques, such as word clouds or sentiment analysis. There are two subcategories of qualitative analysis. They are,

- **Nominal:** This type of data is used for labelling variables and sometimes nominal data is referred to as "labels". The term nominal comes from "nomen" which means "name". E.g., Marital Status, Gender, Hair Color, Ethnicity.

- **Ordinal:** Ordinal data is a type of qualitative data that represents variables that can be ordered or ranked based on their magnitude or degree of a certain attribute. In ordinal data, the order in which the values are present is critical; yet, the distinctions between them are not guaranteed to be meaningful or consistent. Examples of ordinal data include rankings, ratings, grades, and levels of agreement or satisfaction. Ordinal data can be analyzed using non-parametric statistical methods like normal distribution model, linear regression model etc and visualized using bar charts, histograms, or box plots.

Quantitative or Numerical Data: can be represented as a number or can be quantified. It answers key questions such as "how many, how much, and how often". In general, there are two types of data in quantitative or numerical data. They are,

- **Discrete Data:** Data that can only take on specific, distinct values is considered discrete. These values are typically integers or whole numbers and cannot be broken down into smaller units. For example, the number of children in a family is a discrete variable, as it can only take on certain numbers such as 1, 2, 3, etc. Some instances of discrete data include the quantity of items sold, the number of employees in a company, or the number of cars in a parking lot. Discrete data is often analyzed using frequency tables or bar charts to display the frequency of each value.

- **Continuous Data:** Continuous data refers to data that can have any value within a predetermined range or timeframe. The continuous data can take on an infinite number of possible values. We often analyze continuous data using statistical methods such as regression analysis, hypothesis testing, and analysis of variance (ANOVA). Examples of continuous data are speed of the car, the height of the child, the time required to complete a project, and the operating speed of the processor.

4. Define Data Visualization

ANSWER The graphical depiction of information and data is what is known as "data visualization." It includes the use of visual elements like charts, graphs, and maps to present complex data in a simple and intuitive way. The goal of data visualization is to make it easier for people to understand the data and identify patterns and insights that might be difficult to identify from raw data. Effective data visualization requires a combination of technical skills, creativity, and an understanding of the audience and their needs. There are various tools and technologies available for data visualization, including Excel, Tableau, and Python's Matplotlib library.

5. Explain Dataset.

ANSWER   A dataset is a collection of organized and structured data. It can consist of various types of information, such as numbers, text, images, or any other format that can be stored digitally. Datasets are typically used in research, analysis, and machine learning tasks, where the data is examined to uncover patterns, trends, or relationships. Depending on the context, a dataset could represent anything from a simple spreadsheet containing a list of numbers to a complex database containing millions of records with interconnected information.

6. Define population and sample in statistics

ANSWER   In statistics and machine learning, the concepts of population and sample are fundamental to understanding data analysis and modeling.

1. **Population:**
    a. In statistics, a population refers to the entire set of individuals, items, or events that are of interest to the researcher or analyst. It represents the larger group from which a sample is drawn.
    b. For example, if you're studying the heights of all adult males in a country, the population would be all adult males in that country.
2. **Sample:**
    a. A sample is a subset of the population, selected for analysis or study. It's chosen in such a way that it represents the characteristics of the population from which it is drawn.
    b. Using the previous example, if you were to measure the heights of a randomly selected group of 100 adult males from the country, that group would be your sample.

7. Define Distribution

ANSWER In statistics, a distribution refers to the way values are spread out or distributed in a dataset. It describes the frequency of different values or ranges of values that occur in a population or sample. A distribution can be described using many measures, such as mean, median, mode, variance, and standard deviation. Common types of distributions include normal, binomial, Poisson, and exponential distributions, each with its own set of characteristics and applications. Understanding distributions is important for making statistical inferences and drawing conclusions from data.

8. Describe and explain the various types of data measurement scales.

ANSWER The 4 main types of data measurement scales are: ratio, interval, ordinal, and nominal.
- **Nominal data** is categorical data that cannot be ranked, but can be counted and grouped into categories. An example would be the color of a car, as it cannot be ranked but can be grouped into categories such as red or blue.
- **Ordinal data** represents variables that can be ranked or ordered based on their magnitude or degree of a certain attribute. Examples of ordinal data include rankings of customer satisfaction or level of education.

- **Interval data** is a type of quantitative data where the values are ordered and have a constant and equal interval between them. In interval data, the difference between two values is meaningful and consistent across the entire scale, but there is no true zero point. This means that while you can perform arithmetic operations such as addition and subtraction on interval data, you cannot meaningfully perform multiplication or division. Examples include temperature, time, and IQ scores.
- **Ratio data** is a type of quantitative data that has all the properties of interval data, but with an additional feature: a true zero point. In ratio data, the zero point represents a complete absence of the measured attribute, and ratios of values are meaningful.

Understanding the different types of data measurement scales is important when selecting appropriate data visualization methods and statistical analysis.

9. **What do you understand by Central tendency?**

ANSWER Central tendency refers to a statistical measure that indicates the center or typical value of a set of data points. It provides a single value around which the data tend to cluster. The central tendency is used to summarize the main characteristics of a dataset and understand its overall distribution. There are three common measures of central tendency mean, median, and mode.

10. Define Variability

ANSWER Variability, in statistics, refers to the degree of dispersion or spread of a set of data points around their central tendency. It quantifies how much the individual values in a dataset deviate from the typical or average value, providing insight into the diversity or consistency within the data. There are several measures of variability commonly used in statistics. They are range, variance, standard deviation, and interquartile range.

11. Compare Data Measurement Scales

ANSWER

Data Measurement Scales	Measure property	Operations Performed	Advanced operations	Central tendency	Variability
Nominal	Classification, membership	=, ≠	Grouping	Mode	Qualitative variation
Ordinal	Comparison, level	>, <	Sorting	Median	Range, Interquartile range
Interval	Difference, affinity	+, −	Comparison to a standard	Arithmetic mean	Deviation
Ratio	Magnitude, amount	×, /	Ratio	Geometric mean, Harmonic mean	Coefficient of variation, Standard deviation, Interquartile Range

12. **Determine whether the data below are nominal, ordinal, interval, or ratios. Justify your decision.**

a. The average monthly temperature in Fahrenheit degrees for Bengaluru throughout the year.

b. Each player's assigned uniform number on a sports team

ANSWER

a. The average monthly temperature in Fahrenheit degrees for Bengaluru throughout the year → **INTERVAL DATA**

We are collecting interval data when we measure temperature in degrees Fahrenheit or degrees Celsius since the zero points in these systems are not standardised. Temperatures below zero, whether in Fahrenheit or Celsius, are possible.

b. Each player's assigned uniform number on a sports team → **NOMINAL DATA**

The data are categorized using numbers, but no mathematical computations could be made.

13. **What is Exploratory Data Analysis?**

ANSWER Exploratory Data Analysis (EDA) is a method to analyse and understand the data that involves summarizing its key features visually and numerically. It involves using various data visualization techniques, such as histograms, scatter plots, and box plots, to identify patterns, trends, and outliers in the data. EDA is often used as a preliminary step in data analysis to gain insights into the data and to guide further analysis. It can help identify potential problems with the data, such as missing values or outliers, that may need to be addressed before conducting more formal statistical analysis.

CHAPTER 2

STATISTICS

1 **Differentiate between correlation and covariance in statistics**

ANSWER Covariance and correlation are two statistical measures used to describe the relationship between two variables. While they are related, they have some key differences:

Parameter	Covariance	Correlation
Definition	The covariance of two variables is a statistical measure that shows how they vary together. It is the measure of the joint variability of two random variables. In other words, it measures how two variables move with respect to each other.	Correlation is a statistical measure that describes the extent to which two variables are related or move together in a systematic manner. It quantifies the strength and direction of the relationship between variables. It is a normalized version of covariance, which means it is scaled to always fall between -1 and +1.
Range	The range of covariance is unrestricted and can range from negative infinity to positive infinity. This makes it difficult to interpret the magnitude of the covariance.	Correlation ranges from -1 to +1, making it easier to interpret. Perfect linear relationships are represented by correlations of -1 for negative relationships, 0 for no linear relationships, and +1 for positive relationships.

Statistics

Interpretation	Covariance can be difficult to interpret because it does not have a standardized scale. A covariance that is positive implies the variables tend to move in the same direction, while a covariance that is negative shows that the variables move in opposing directions. However, the magnitude of the covariance does not tell us how strong the relationship is.	Correlation provides an easy-to-understand interpretation of the relationship between two variables. It tells us both the direction and strength of the relationship.
Calculation	The formula for calculating covariance involves multiplying each variable's standard deviation away from its own mean and then finding the average of the product that this process produces. $$Covariance\ (x,y) = \frac{1}{N-1}\sum_{i=1}^{N}(x_i - \bar{x})(y_i - \bar{y})$$ Where covariance (x,y) = covariance between x and y x_i = data value of x y_i = data value of y $\bar{x}$ = mean of x $\bar{y}$ = mean of y N = number of data values	The correlation is found by taking the covariance and dividing it by the product of the standard deviations of the two variables. $$\rho_{xy} = Correlation\ (x,y)$$ $$= \frac{\Sigma(x_i - \bar{x})(y_i - \bar{y})}{\sqrt{\Sigma(x_i - \bar{x})^2 \Sigma(y_i - \bar{y})^2}}$$ Where ρ_{xy} = correlation coefficient x_i = values of the x-variable in a sample $\bar{x}$ = mean of the values of the x-variable y_i = values of the y-variable in a sample $\bar{y}$ = mean of the values of the y-variable

Applications of Covariance

I. Covariance is used in Genetics and Molecular Biology to measure the genetic relationship matrix.
II. It is used in the prediction of investment amount of different assets in financial markets.
III. Covariance is used to collate the data from astronomical / oceanographic studies to arrive at a final conclusion.
IV. It is used to analyse a set of data with logical implications of the principal component.
V. It is used to study signals obtained in various forms.

Applications of Correlation

I. Time vs Money spent by a customer on online e-commerce websites.
II. It is used to compare the previous records of weather forecast to the current year.
III. Correlation is widely used in pattern recognition.
IV. To analyse the raise in temperature during summer and its impact on the consumption of water amongst the family members.
V To gauge the relationship between the population and poverty.

2   **Define Variance.**

ANSWER   In statistics, variance is a measure of how scattered a collection of data is. It is determined as the average of the squared deviations of each data point from the data set's mean.

The formula for variance is as follows:

$$\sigma^2 = \frac{1}{N}\sum (X - \mu)^2$$

Where
(μ) mean = is the average of the data set
N = is the number of data points
X = is the value of each data point.

To put it another way, variance is just the average of the squared standard deviations. It is used to measure how much variability or dispersion there is in a collection of data.

When the variance is high, the data points are dispersed throughout a broad range of values, but when the variance is low, the data points are tightly packed around the mean. In statistical analysis, variability is often used to evaluate a data set's range and to compare the variability of several data sets.

3 What are the uses of Probability Density function.

ANSWER The probability density function (PDF) is a vital concept in probability theory and statistics that has numerous uses, some of which include:

- **Describing the probability distribution of a continuous random variable:** The PDF provides a way to describe the likelihood of different values of a continuous random variable. It is a mathematical function that explains the probability of various outcomes or values that a random variable might have.

- **Calculating probabilities:** The PDF can calculate the probability that a continuous random variable takes on a particular value or falls within a certain range of values. This is done by integrating the PDF across the necessary value range.
- **Calculating summary statistics:** The PDF can calculate summary statistics such as the mean, variance, and standard deviation of a continuous random variable. These statistics are important in various fields, including physics, engineering, and finance.
- **Modeling real-world phenomena:** Probability density functions are used to model many real-world phenomena, such as the heights of people in a population, the amount of rainfall in a particular region, or the time it takes for a customer to complete a transaction in a store.
- **Hypothesis testing:** The PDF can be used in hypothesis testing to determine whether a particular data set is consistent with a given distribution. This is an important tool in statistical inference, which is used to make predictions (whether the sample evidence supports or contradicts the hypothesis) and draw conclusions from data.

Overall, the probability density function is a powerful tool in probability theory and statistics that is used in a wide range of applications, from modeling real-world phenomena to making predictions and drawing conclusions from data.

4 Mention the mathematical equation to calculate the Standard Deviation?

ANSWER In statistics, the standard deviation is a measure of the spread of a set of data from its mean (average) value and it is a key tool in statistical analysis for describing the variability in a data set and comparing different data sets.
Standard Deviation is calculated using the formula.

$$Standard\ Deviation = \sqrt{\frac{\sum_{i=1}^{N}(x_i - \bar{x})}{N}}$$

Where
N = represents the total number of data points
x_i = represents each individual data point
$\bar{x}$ = represents the mean of the dataset

The standard deviation is an important tool in statistical analysis because it provides a way to quantify the variability in a data set and to compare the variability of different data sets. It is commonly used to calculate confidence intervals and to assess the significance of differences between data sets.

5 Define Probability Mass Function

ANSWER A probability mass function (PMF) is a function that describes the probability distribution of a discrete random variable. It assigns probabilities to each possible value that the random variable can take.

For a discrete random variable X, the probability mass function P[X=x] gives the probability that X is equal to a specific value x.

Mathematically, a PMF is denoted as
$$f(x) = P[X = x]$$
PMF must satisfy two conditions:

$f(x) \geq 0$ for all $x \in S$

$\sum_{x \in S} f(x) = 1$, where the sum is taken over all possible values of X.

6 Explain Probability Density Function (PDF)

ANSWER In statistics, a density function (also called probability density function or PDF) is a mathematical function that represents the likelihood of various values in a random variable.

The density function is non-negative and integrates to 1 over the entire range of possible values of the random variable. It provides a way to calculate the probability of a random variable falling within a certain range of values, by integrating the density function over that range.

The density function is often used in statistical analysis to describe the distribution of a random variable. Common examples of density functions include the normal distribution, the binomial distribution, and the Poisson distribution. The density function can calculate summary statistics such as mean, median, and mode, and to compare different distributions.

Mathematically, the probability of X falling within a certain interval [a,b] is given by the integral of the PDF over that interval represented as below.

$$\Pr[a \leq X \leq b] = \int_a^b f_X(x)dx$$

7. What does a high Standard Deviation indicate?

ANSWER A high standard deviation as shown in figure 2.1(b) indicates that the set's data points are more spread out from the mean value of the set. The values in the data set are more diverse and have a wider range of variability in a high standard deviation.

A large standard deviation specifies that the data points are further away from the mean value, and that there is more uncertainty or unpredictability in the data. This is in contrast to a small standard deviation as shown in figure 2.1(a), which indicates that the data points are closer to the mean value, and there is less variability and more consistency in the data.

For example, if the average height of a group of people is five feet ten inches, and the standard deviation is four inches, this shows that the heights of the individuals in the group are widely dispersed around the mean value. Some people in the group may be much taller or much shorter than the average height, while others may be closer to the mean.

Figure 2.1(a & b) : Small Standard Deviation and Large Standard Deviation

8 In what ways are you familiar with the concept of normal distribution?

ANSWER Normal distribution (known as Gaussian distribution), is a probability distribution in statistical analysis. It is a symmetrical bell-shaped curve centred on the data set's mean (average) value. The form of the curve is governed by two parameters: the mean and the standard deviation as shown in figure 2.2.

The normal distribution is characterized by the following properties:

- **Symmetry:** The normal distribution is symmetrical around the mean value, which is also the point of maximum probability.
- **Bell-shaped curve:** The shape of the normal distribution is a smooth, bell-shaped curve that is symmetrical around the mean value.
- **Empirical rule:** According to the empirical rule, which is followed by the normal distribution, about 68.1% of the data will fall within one standard deviation of the mean, 95.5% of the data will fall within two standard deviations of the mean, and 99.7% of the data will fall within three standard deviations of the mean.

The normal distribution is widely used in statistical analysis because various natural phenomena and measurements tend to follow this distribution. For example, the heights of people in a population, the weights of objects, and the IQ scores of individuals are often normally distributed.

The normal distribution is also used as a theoretical model in many statistical tests and analyses. It offers a valuable outline for understanding and analyzing the distribution of data, and it is a key tool in hypothesis testing and confidence interval estimation.

The general form of its probability density function(pdf) is

$$f(x) = \frac{1}{\sigma\sqrt{2\pi}}\, e^{-\frac{1}{2}\left(\frac{x-\mu}{\sigma}\right)^2}$$

Where x = any random variable
    μ = mean
    σ = standard deviation

when μ = 0 and variance/ standard deviation = 1, it becomes Standard Normal Distribution.

$$f(x) = \frac{e^{-\frac{x^2}{2}}}{\sqrt{2\pi}}$$

The term "normal deviation" is used to describe a random variable that follows the Gaussian distribution. Informally, a bell curve can refer to a normal distribution.

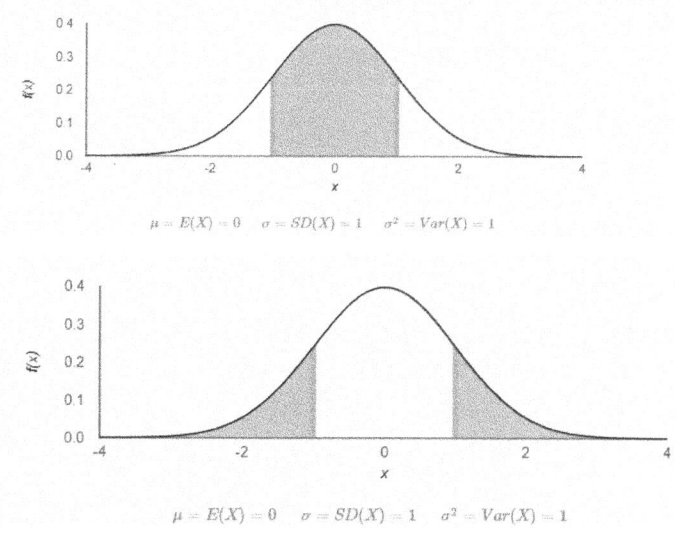

Figure 2.2: A plot of normal distribution (or bell-shaped curve) where each band has a width of 1 standard deviation

In the above figure, μ is mean, σ is standard deviation and σ2 is variance.

9   Define Median. How can you calculate the median?

ANSWER   In statistics, the median is a measure of central tendency that signifies the mid value of a data set when the data is arranged in order of magnitude. For the calculation of the median, the data is first arranged in order from smallest to largest (or largest to smallest), and then the middle value is identified.

If n is odd,

$$median(x) = x_{\frac{(n+1)}{2}}$$

If the number of observations in the data set is odd, then the median is simply the middle observation.

For example, in the data set {1, 2, 3, 4, 5}, the median is 3 because it is the middle value.

If n is even,

$$median(x) = \frac{x_{\frac{n}{2}} + x_{\frac{n}{2}+1}}{2}$$

If the number of observations in the data set is even, then the median is calculated as the average of the two middle observations.

For example, in the data set {1, 2, 3, 4, 5, 6}, the median is (3+4)/2 = 3.5.

The median is often used as a measure of central tendency when the data contains outliers or extreme values that can skew the mean (average) value of the data. Unlike the mean, the median is not influenced by extreme values in the data set, and it provides a more robust measure of the central tendency.

10 What are outliers in statistics?

ANSWER In statistics, an outlier is an observation or data point that is significantly different from other observations in a data set as indicated in figure 2.3. Outliers can occur due to various reasons, such as measurement errors, data entry errors, or genuine variability in the data.

Figure 2.3: Example of an outlier with data value having different features

Outliers can have a significant impact on the analysis and interpretation of data, as they can skew the results and lead to inaccurate conclusions. For example, in a data set of exam scores, an outlier representing an extremely high score could lead to the conclusion that the entire group performed exceptionally well, when in fact the majority of scores may have been average.

It is important to identify and handle outliers appropriately in statistical analysis. One approach is to use statistical methods such as box plots or z-scores to identify potential outliers. Once identified, the researcher can then decide whether to remove the outlier from the analysis, or to analyze the data with and without the outlier to assess its impact on the results.

In some cases, outliers may represent genuine variability in the data, and removing them may not be appropriate. In such cases, it may be necessary to investigate the cause of the outlier and consider alternative statistical methods that are robust to outliers, such as non-parametric methods.

11 Explain the different types of outliers

ANSWER There are several types of outliers that can occur in a data set
- **Point outliers:** These are individual data points that are significantly different from other observations in the data set.
- **Contextual outliers:** These are data points that are considered outliers only in a particular context or sub-group of the data. For example, a high-income earner may be an outlier in a group of low-income earners, but not in a larger population.
- **Collective outliers:** These are groups or clusters of data points that are significantly different from the rest of the data set. These can occur due to errors in data collection or due to genuine differences in the data.
- **Masking outliers:** These are data points that are not identified as outliers when analyzed independently, but become apparent when analyzed in combination with other data.
- **Swamping outliers:** These are data points that are identified as outliers, but may not actually be significantly different from the rest of the dataset due to the presence of other, more extreme outliers.

Identifying and understanding the type of outlier is important for appropriate handling of the data. While some outliers may need to be removed or adjusted, others may provide valuable information about the data or indicate underlying patterns or relationships.

12 Explain different methods to find outliers

ANSWER There are several methods to identify outliers in a dataset. Some common methods include:

- **Box plots:** Box plots, also known as box-and-whisker plots, provide a visual representation of the data distribution, including outliers. The box represents the middle 50% of the data, and the whiskers extend to the minimum and maximum values within a specified range. Any data points outside the whiskers are considered outliers.

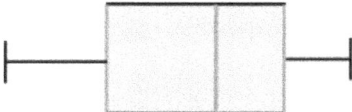

- **Z-scores:** Z-scores represent the number of standard deviations a data point is from the mean. Data points with a z-score greater than a specified threshold (usually 2 or 3) are considered outliers.
- **Tukey's method:** This method defines outliers as data points that fall outside the range of 1.5 times the interquartile range (IQR) below the first quartile or above the third quartile.
- **Mahalanobis distance:** This method calculates the distance between each data point and the mean of the data set, considering the covariance between variables. Data points with a high Mahalanobis distance are considered outliers.
- **Local outlier factor (LOF):** This method calculates the density of data points in a neighborhood around each point and identifies outliers as points with a significantly lower density than their neighbors.

- **Cluster analysis:** Outliers can also be identified using clustering algorithms that group similar data points together. Points that do not fit into any cluster may be considered outliers.

It is important to note that no single method is perfect for identifying all types of outliers, and the choice of method may depend on the nature of the data and the research question. Additionally, outliers should not always be removed from the analysis, as they may provide important information or indicate underlying patterns in the data. It is important to carefully consider the reasons for any outliers and to handle them appropriately in the analysis.

13 What are sampling and various methods of sampling?

ANSWER Sampling is the process of selecting a subset of individuals, objects, or observations from a larger population to estimate or understand characteristics of the whole population as depicted in figure 2.4. In statistical analysis, sampling is an important tool for making inferences about a population using a smaller, more manageable sample.

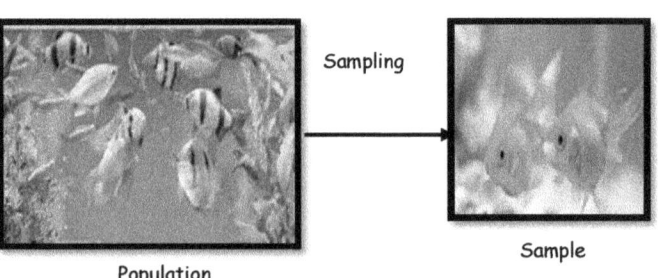

Figure 2.4: Illustration of Sampling

Need for Sampling:

Sampling is an essential tool for statistical analysis and research in numerous fields, including social sciences, market research, and healthcare. There are several reasons sampling is necessary:

- **Cost-effectiveness:** It is often impractical or too expensive to collect data from an entire population. Sampling provides a more efficient way of collecting data by selecting a smaller subset of individuals or objects to represent the whole population.
- **Time-saving:** Collecting data from an entire population can be time-consuming, whereas sampling can provide a quicker way to collect data and get results.
- **Accuracy:** Sampling can provide accurate estimates of population characteristics if done properly. Many times, a well-designed sample can provide results that are just as accurate as those got from a full population census.
- **Feasibility:** Sometimes, it may be impossible to conduct a full census of a population, for example, when the population is constantly changing or is spread out over a large geographic area.
- **Practicality:** Sampling allows researchers to work with a manageable amount of data, making it easier to analyze and draw meaningful conclusions.

Overall, sampling is an important tool for obtaining accurate, reliable, and practical data from a population, while saving time and costs. However, it is important to use appropriate sampling techniques and carefully consider any potential biases in the sample to ensure that the results are valid and representative of the population.

Different Types of Sampling Techniques

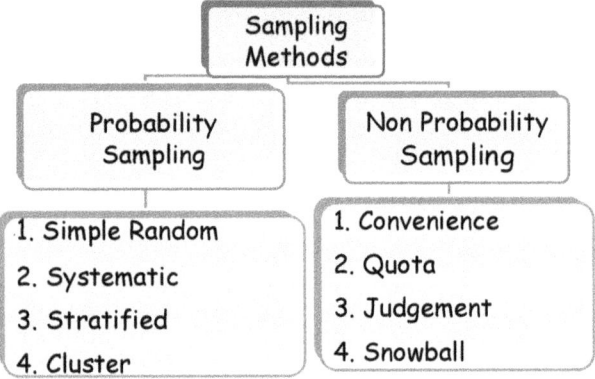

Figure 2.5: Hierarchy of Sampling Methods

The best technique relies on the data set and circumstance. There are various approaches for extracting samples from data, as shown in figure 2.5.

Probability Sampling

By assigning random numbers to points in the data collection, probability-based sampling can be used to make sure that there is no connection between the points chosen for the sample. This lets the user make strong statistical inferences about the whole group. There is equal probability of selecting any individual member of the population. Other probability sampling variations include:

- **Simple Random Sampling:** There is an equal chance that each subset of a sampling frame will be chosen in a simple random sample (SRS) of a given size. The sample should include the whole population. Methods like random number generator, physical methods like flipping coins and using dice can be used. It works best when there is sufficient time and funding for the study or when the data set is small.
- **Stratified Sampling:** Stratified sampling is categorizing individuals into mutually exclusive categories and then selecting members from those groups using basic random sampling. Stratified sampling produces strata or layers that are remarkably typical of layers or strata in the population. This sampling helps to guarantee that all of the population's subgroups have equal representation while also reducing the researcher's potential for bias. It takes a lot of time, does not account for all the variations among the population's subgroups, and making strata for the sample is challenging.
- **Systematic Sampling:** A researcher can identify members of the research population using systematic sampling, a probability sampling technique, which uses a random beginning point and defined intervals. It is easy to implement but may lead to biased results if patterns exists in the data.
- **Cluster Sampling:** Researchers can gather data using the cluster sampling approach by grouping the whole population into clusters that each represent a population. If the cluster members are not homogenous, it might not function well.

Uses of Probability Sampling
- It is cost effective
- It is simple and straight forward
- It is non-technical: This does not require any technical knowledge because of its simplicity

Nonprobability sampling is another way in which a data sample is chosen and extracted depending on the analyst's judgement. Because the analyst selects inclusion, extrapolating whether the sample correctly represents the wider population might be more challenging than when probability sampling is used. Types of non-probability sampling includes

- **Convenience Sampling:** This sampling is based on subject accessibility, such as polling consumers in a mall or pedestrians on a bustling street. It is sometimes referred to as convenience sampling due to the ease with which the researcher can conduct it and contact the individuals.
- **Snowball Sampling:** A snowball sample works by bringing in a few sample participants, who then bring in additional participants they know. Using the snowball technique proves effective in reaching highly targeted populations, many of whom are likely to be acquainted with individuals meeting the criteria.
- **Quota Sampling:** After separating the population into subgroups based on characteristics such as age or geography, quota sampling establishes objectives for the number of respondents required from each segment. The main difference between quota and stratified random sampling is that quota sampling does not use a random sample approach.

- **Judgmental Sampling:** The sample selection in a purposive or judgmental sampling approach is left to the researcher and their knowledge of who would fulfil the study requirements.

Uses of Non-Probability Sampling

- Researchers find non-probability sampling methods easier to use in real-world surveys.
- Non-probability sampling produces findings faster and cheaper since the researcher knows the sample.

14 Show how to choose a simple random sample from a population

ANSWER Any combination has an equal chance of being chosen in a simple random sample, which is a sample that is chosen at random. For example, a basic random sample would choose three of the six colored balls from an urn that contains them without looking at it.

15 How should a cluster sample be chosen from a population?

ANSWER The population is initially divided into groups, known as clusters, and then randomly selected clusters are included in the sample. It is possible to choose the whole cluster or only a section of it at random.

For instance, if a researcher wants to survey a sample of mall patrons, he / she might pick a few stores at random and then only speak with the patrons inside those stores. The clusters in this illustration are the stores.

Each cluster chosen for the sample must represent the entire population in order for cluster sampling to be successful.

16 What is skewness?

ANSWER The meaning of skewness is lack of symmetry. Skewness is a measure of the asymmetry of a probability distribution. It measures the degree to which a distribution is skewed or distorted from a symmetrical distribution. A distribution can be positively skewed, negatively skewed, or approximately symmetrical.

Negative Skew (left-skewed, left-tailed, or skewed to the left)

In a negatively skewed distribution, the tail of the distribution is longer on the left side than on the right side. This means that there are more values on the right side of the distribution that are closer to the median, and fewer values on the left side of the distribution that are farther away from the median as shown in figure 2. 6.

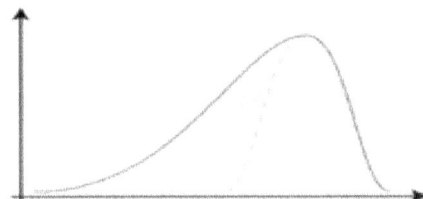

Figure 2. 6: Negative Skew Distribution

Positive Skew (right-skewed, right-tailed, or skewed to the right)

In a positively skewed distribution, the tail of the distribution is longer on the right side than on the left side. This means that there are more values on the left side of the distribution that are closer to the median, and fewer values on the right side of the distribution that are farther away from the median as shown in figure 2. 7.

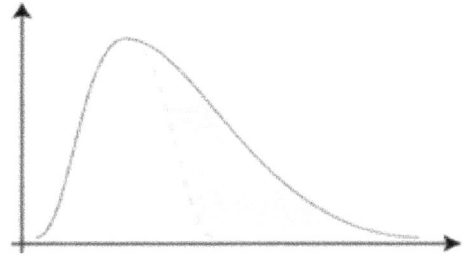

Figure 2. 7: Positive Skew Distribution

The skewness of a distribution can be calculated using a formula that involves the mean, median, and standard deviation of the distribution. A skewness value of zero indicates a perfectly symmetrical distribution as depicted in figure 2. 8. Positive skewness values indicate a positively skewed distribution, and negative skewness values indicate a negatively skewed distribution.

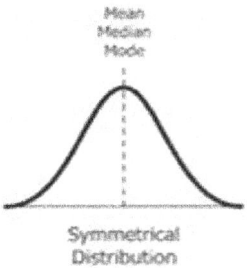

Figure 2. 8: Zero Skew Distribution

 **Advantages of using Skewness**
- Skewness provides a more precise measure of the performance of investment returns.
- It is an often-used technique in statistics since it enables one to determine how much of the data deviates from the normal distribution.

17 Describe Kurtosis

ANSWER Kurtosis is used to describe distribution. Kurtosis is a statistical measure that describes the shape of a probability distribution's tail. It is a measure of the degree to which a distribution is more or less peaked than the normal distribution. A distribution can be leptokurtic (tall and thin), mesokurtic (bell-shaped like a normal distribution), or platykurtic (flat and broad) as represented in figure 2.9.

There are three types of kurtosis:

Leptokurtic distributions have a higher peak than a normal distribution and heavy tails. Mesokurtic distributions have a peak and tails that are similar to a normal distribution. Platykurtic distributions have a lower peak than a normal distribution and light tails.

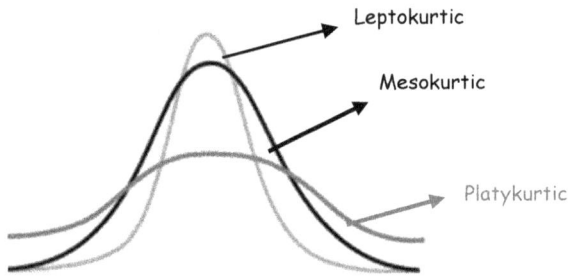

Figure 2. 9: Types of Kurtosis

The kurtosis of a distribution can be calculated using a formula that involves the fourth central moment and the variance of the distribution. A kurtosis value of zero indicates a perfectly normal distribution. Positive kurtosis values indicate a leptokurtic distribution, and negative kurtosis values indicate a platykurtic distribution.

$$Kurt[X] = \frac{\mu_4}{\sigma^4}$$

Where μ_4 = is the fourth central moment
σ = is the standard deviation.

It is important to note that kurtosis is not a measure of the spread or variability of the distribution, but rather a measure of the shape of the distribution's tails.

18 Explain the Pareto Principle

ANSWER The Pareto principle, also known as the 80/20 rule, is a concept that states that approximately 80% of the effects come from 20% of the causes.

The Pareto principle has since been applied to many different fields, including business, economics, and personal productivity. The fact that this theory practically applies to everything in our environment makes it so intriguing:

- 20% of the donors contribute 80% of the total
- 80% of healthcare costs are often caused by 20% of patients
- 20% of the code has 80% of the errors
- 80% of the world's wealth rests with 20% of the people
- 80% of the value of a project often comes from the first 20% of effort
- 20% of your clients will give you 80% of the business
- 80% of time spent with friends, is with only 20% of them
- 20% of the drivers cause 80% of all traffic accidents

While the numbers 80/20 are not necessarily exact, the Pareto principle highlights the fact that a minority of causes or inputs often have a disproportionate impact on the outcomes or outputs. By identifying and focusing on the most important factors, individuals and organizations can achieve greater efficiency and effectiveness in their work.

19 **Outline the steps to find the mean length of all the fishes in the sea.**

ANSWER   Here are the general steps to find the mean length of all the fishes in the sea:
- **Define the population:** Determine the population of all the fishes in the sea whose mean length you want to calculate. This may be an entire ocean or a specific region within an ocean.
- **Determine the sample:** Decide on the sample of fishes whose lengths will be measured. The sample should be demonstrative of the entire people, and the sample size should be large enough to ensure accuracy.
- **Collect the data:** Collect the length measurements for all the fishes in the sample. Ensure that the measurements are accurate and consistent.
- **Compute the sample mean:** Sum up all the length measurements and divide by the sample size to find the sample mean. This is an estimate of the mean length of the fishes in the population.
- **Consider the population characteristics:** Determine if the sample mean is a good estimate of the population mean by considering the population's characteristics. For example, if the population is normally distributed, the sample mean may be a good estimate of the population mean.
- **Calculate the population mean:** If the sample mean is a good estimate of the population mean, use it as the estimate of the mean length of all the fishes in the sea. If not, more data may need to be collected or other statistical methods may need to be used to estimate the population mean.

- **Report the results:** Once the mean length of all the fishes in the sea has been estimated, report the results with appropriate measures of precision, such as confidence intervals or standard errors

20 **What is the probability of selecting a fish at random that weighs over 1 kg, considering the provided mean (0.8) and standard deviation values (0.3)?**

ANSWER
- Based on the input given, the dispersal of weights of fish is normally distributed with a mean (μ) of 0.8 kg and a standard deviation (σ) of 0.3
- Calculate z-score by replacing X with 1. (1-0.8)/0.3=0.6667
- Investigate p table values and determine p(z>0.6667) = 0.252
- Based on the normality assumption, the probability that a randomly selected fish weighing more than one kilogram is roughly about 25.2%

21 **Describe how the standard error and margin of error are related.**

ANSWER The standard error and margin of error are both statistical measures used to estimate the precision of an estimate or sample statistic. While they are related, they are not the same thing.

The dispersion or randomness of a sample statistic may be quantified by calculating its standard error. It measures how much the sample statistic is likely to vary from the true population parameter. Typically, the standard error is calculated by dividing the standard deviation of the sample statistic by the square root of the sample size. If the sample statistic has a lower standard error, it suggests that the sample statistic's estimate of the population parameter is more accurate.

The margin of error, on the other hand, is a measure of the uncertainty or level of precision of an estimate or sample statistic. It is a representation of the value range that the real population parameter is most likely to fall inside, based on the data obtained from the sample. The margin of error is typically calculated as a multiple of the standard error, based on a specified level of confidence. The margin of error also grows in proportion to the standard error.

22 What must we know prior to pursuing data analysis?

ANSWER Before pursuing data analysis, there are several things that we should know or consider:

The research question: We should clearly understand of the research question or problem that we are trying to address with the data analysis. This will guide our choice of data sources, variables, and statistical methods.

The data sources: We should know the sources of data that we will use for the analysis. This includes knowing the type of data (e.g., categorical, numerical), the format of the data (e.g., spreadsheets, databases), and any limitations or biases in the data.

Data quality: We should assess the quality of the data, including any missing values, errors, or outliers. This may involve cleaning and preprocessing the data before analysis.

Variables: We should identify and define the variables that will be used in the analysis. This includes deciding on the type of variable (e.g., continuous, categorical), the units of measurement, and the operational definitions.

Statistical methods: We should select appropriate statistical methods based on the research question, data sources, and variables. This may involve conducting descriptive statistics, inferential statistics, distributions, hypothesis testing, regression analysis, or other techniques.

Software tools: We should be familiar with the software tools that will be used for the analysis, such as statistical software, spreadsheets, or programming languages.

Ethical considerations: We should consider any ethical implications of the data analysis, such as protecting privacy and confidentiality, avoiding biases, and ensuring that the results are communicated clearly and accurately.

By considering these above factors before pursuing data analysis, we can ensure that the analysis is appropriate, valid, and useful for addressing the research question or problem at hand.

23 Describe a root cause analysis example

ANSWER

As the name implies, root cause analysis is a method of problem solving that begins with finding the root cause of the problem.

A retail store notices that their shelves are frequently out of stock. Root Cause Analysis is conducted to identify the root cause, and it is discovered that the store's ordering process is inadequate, leading to frequent ordering delays.

24 Define Central Tendency

ANSWER The term "central tendency" comes from the field of statistics and describes the value that is most representative of an entire group of numbers. It is often used to summarize the data by describing a single value that represents the entire set. There are several measures of central tendency as shown in figure 2.10, including:

1) **Mean:** Adding up all the values in the dataset, then dividing that sum by the total number of values, yields the mean value for the dataset. The mean is affected by outliers and is not always representative of the entire dataset.

2) **Median:** When the values are ranked from least to greatest, the value that represents the median of the dataset is the one that is in the centre. It is not affected by outliers and is often used when the data is skewed.

3) **Mode:** The mode is the most frequent value in the dataset. It is often used when the data is categorical or when identifying the most common value is important.

Each measure of central tendency has its strengths and weaknesses and is appropriate for diverse types of data and research questions. It is essential to give serious consideration to the data and the research question when selecting a measure of central tendency.

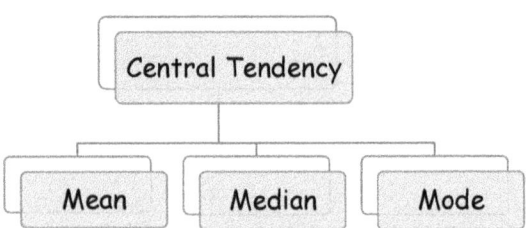

Figure 2.10: Several measures of Central Tendency

25	**Discuss the need for Dispersion. Explain the two methods to measure the degree of variation present in the dataset**
ANSWER	Dispersion is used to calculate the variability of data or to determine how spread out the data is. It determines how much the scores in a distribution deviate from the average score. The measure of data is done in statistics by using Central Tendency and Dispersion. The 2 important types of dispersion used in statistics are:

- **Absolute Measure of Dispersion:** Absolute measures of dispersion are statistical measures that define the spread of data in similar units as the original data, without considering the direction of deviation from the central value. These measures are not affected by the presence of outliers and are more appropriate when handling ordinal or interval data. It contains information such as range, standard deviation, quartile deviation, and others.
- **Relative Measure of Dispersion:** Relative measures of dispersion are statistical measures that describe the spread of data relative to the central value, and are expressed as ratios or percentages. These measures are useful when comparing the variability of data sets with different means, or when working with data that has different units of measurement. Some common techniques for relative dispersion are:
  - Range
  - Variation
  - Standard Deviation
  - Quartile Deviation
  - Mean Deviation

26   What do you understand by Hypothesis?

ANSWER   In statistics, a hypothesis is a tentative statement or claim that is subject to further testing and verification. It is an assertion or conjecture about the relationship between two or more variables and is typically based on prior knowledge, observations, or theories. Hypotheses are used in scientific research to guide the collection and analysis of data and to draw conclusions about the nature of the relationships between variables.

27   Define Hypothesis Testing

ANSWER   According to the evidence from a sample of data, hypothesis testing is a statistical technique used to establish if a hypothesis about a population is likely to be true. The procedure requires the formulation of two competing hypotheses, the null hypothesis and the alternative hypothesis, and the application of statistical methods to determine which hypothesis is supported by the data.

28   A grocery delivery company claims that its average delivery time is less than 15 minutes. State the null and alternative hypotheses that prove this claim.

ANSWER   The alternative hypothesis H_1 represents the claim that the company is attempting to verify - that the mean population of the delivery time is less than 15 minutes. The null hypothesis H_0 is the opposite of H_1 and includes the possibility of equality.

$$H_0: \mu \geq 15 \text{ minutes}$$
$$H_1: \mu < 15 \text{ minutes}$$

29. Bring out the differences between Null Hypothesis and Alternate Hypothesis

ANSWER

Null Hypothesis: The alternative hypothesis, which assumes the opposite of the null hypothesis, states that there is a substantial difference or link between the variables being researched. The default assumption here is that there is no significant difference or relationship between the variables being studied. Hypothesis testing involves calculating a test statistic, such as a t-statistic or z-score, based on the sample data, and comparing it to a critical value based on the chosen significance level and degrees of freedom.

Alternate Hypothesis: The alternative hypothesis in statistics is a statement that says there is a significant difference or relationship between two or more variables being researched. It is the inverse of the null hypothesis, which holds that no substantial difference or link exists between the variables.

The alternative hypothesis is formulated based on prior knowledge, observations, or theories about the nature of the association between the variables being studied. It is typically expressed as a directional or non-directional statement about the expected relationship between the variables.

Example: The mutual fund's average yearly return is 8% every year.

Null Hypothesis: The mutual fund's average return is 8%.

Alternate Hypothesis: The mutual fund's average annual return is not equal to 8% annually.

30 What is the difference between Type I and Type II errors?

ANSWER Type I and Type II errors are two categories of errors that can occur in statistical hypothesis testing.

Type I error occurs when the null hypothesis is rejected even though it is true. In other words, it is a **false positive**. This error is often denoted by the symbol α, and its probability is the significance level of the test. A type I error is considered a more serious error because it leads to false conclusions and wasted resources.

Type II error occurs when the null hypothesis is not rejected even though it is false. In other words, it is a **false negative**. This error is often denoted by the symbol β, and its probability depends on the power of the test. A type II error is also a serious error because it leads to the failure to detect important effects or differences.

Example: A "false positive" is when the key chain gets mistaken for a gun (machine goes beep)

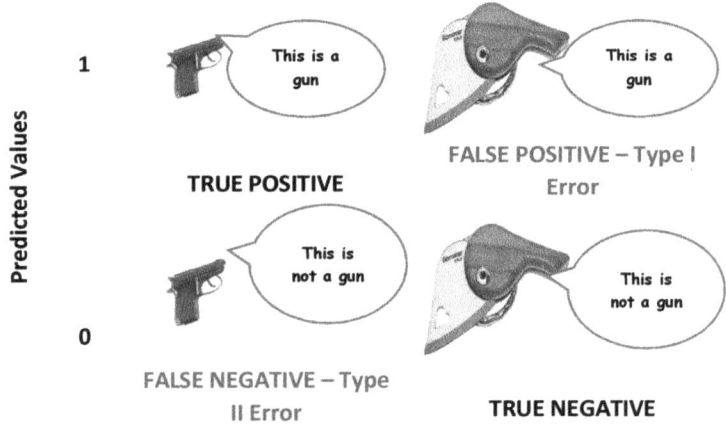

31 Explain Simpson's Paradox

ANSWER When multiple sets of data are joined, a trend that previously existed in those groups vanishes or even reverses—a phenomenon known as Simpson's paradox occurs. This paradox occurs when there is a confounding variable that affects the relationship between the variables being studied and the groups being compared.

For example, suppose we are studying the admission rates of male and female applicants to a university. We find that the overall admission rate for men is lower than the admission rate for women. However, when we break down the data by department, we find that men have a higher admission rate than women in each department. This is an example of Simpson's paradox because the trend of women having a higher admission rate disappears when the groups are combined.

32 For which machine learning solution do you apply hypothesis testing?

ANSWER Hypothesis testing is commonly applied in the evaluation and validation stage of machine learning solutions, particularly in assessing the statistical significance of observed differences or effects. Here are a few scenarios where hypothesis testing is commonly used in machine learning like feature selection, model evaluation, A/B testing, and Anomaly detection.

The hypothesis testing method seeks to infer or reach a conclusion about the total population or set of data. Some assumptions are made to derive two terms: null hypothesis and alternate hypothesis that are employed in the hypothesis testing.

33 Explain p-values. What does P in p-value stand for?

ANSWER In statistics, the p-value is a measure of the evidence against the null hypothesis. If the null hypothesis is correct, it shows the likelihood of having a result that is as severe to or more extreme than the observed outcome.

In hypothesis testing, the p-value is compared to a pre-determined significance level, typically denoted by α, to determine whether the null hypothesis should be rejected or not. The alternative hypothesis is accepted in place of the null hypothesis if the p-value is less than the significance threshold. The null hypothesis is not rejected if the p-value exceeds the significance threshold.

For example, suppose we are testing whether a new drug is effective in treating a particular disease. The alternative hypothesis is that the medicine is effective, as opposed to the null hypothesis that it is ineffective. We conduct a clinical trial and find a p-value of 0.03. If our significance level is 0.05, we would reject the null hypothesis and conclude that the drug is effective, since the p-value is less than the significance level All hypothesis tests ultimately use a p-value to weigh the strength of the evidence. The following explanation applies to the p-value, which is an integer between 0 and 1.

P in p-value stands for Probability Value.

34 Why correlation coefficient is better than covariance as a measure of the relationship between two variables?

ANSWER Covariance and correlation are two methods for determining the association between two variables, however, correlation is preferable because it is unaffected by changes in scale.

35 Define Central Limit Theorem

ANSWER The Central Limit Theorem (CLT) is a fundamental principle in statistics that states that, under certain conditions, the distribution of the sample means of a sufficiently large number of independent and identically distributed random variables will be approximately normally distributed, regardless of the shape of the original population distribution. This theorem is widely used in inferential statistics, particularly in hypothesis testing and confidence interval estimation, as it allows for making inferences about population parameters based on sample data.

The conditions required for the CLT to hold are:
1) The sample is random and independent.
2) The sample size is large enough (typically $n \geq 30$).
3) The population has a finite variance.

The CLT is important because it allows us to make inferences about the population mean using a sample mean, even when the population distribution is unknown or not normal. By taking repeated samples and calculating their means, we can approximate the sampling distribution of the sample means. This sampling distribution will be nearly normal, with the mean of the population serving as its centre, and its standard deviation will be equal to the standard deviation of the population divided by the square root of the size of the sample.

The CLT has important applications in statistical inference, such as hypothesis testing and confidence interval estimation. It also explains why the normal distribution is so commonly observed in various areas of science and social science, even when the underlying population distributions may be non-normal.

36 What universal prerequisites must be met for the central limit theorem to be true?

ANSWER The following prerequisites must be met for the central limit theorem to hold:
- The data must adhere to the randomization criterion so that it must be sampled randomly, for the central limit theorem to hold.
- The sample values must be independent of one another, according to the Independence Assumptions.
- Large sample sizes are required.

37 Why is Central Limit Theorem CLT important?

ANSWER It is important because CLT is used to compute confidence intervals and conduct hypothesis testing.

38 Explain Causation.

ANSWER In a connection between two variables, causation occurs when one of the variables (the cause) is responsible for the change in the other variable (the effect). To establish a causal relationship, several criteria need to be met, including:
- **Temporal precedence:** The cause must occur before the effect.
- **Covariation:** There must be a dependable relationship between the cause and effect across dissimilar individuals, times, and situations.
- **Elimination of alternative explanations:** Other factors that could explain the relationship between the cause and effect must be ruled out.
- **Plausibility:** The proposed causal mechanism must be biologically or theoretically plausible.

Establishing causation is important in numerous fields, including medicine, psychology, and social science, because it allows us to understand how different variables are related and how to intervene to change outcomes. However, establishing causation is not always possible, and in some cases, only a correlational relationship can be inferred. In such cases, it is important to consider the limitations of the data and the possibility of alternative explanations for the observed relationship. **Example:** Heavy alcohol consumption causes an increase in chronic diseases.

39   Why are correlation and causation important?

ANSWER   Correlation and causation are important concepts in statistics and research because they help us understand the relationship between variables and make predictions about how changes in one variable may affect another variable.

For example

- Is there a relationship between heavy alcohol consumption and chronic diseases?
- Is there a correlation between an individual's level of education and their health?
- Is health monitoring associated with living longer?
- Is there a correlation between a company's mobile marketing strategy and an uptick in sales?

These and other queries explore the possibility of a relationship between the two variables, and if one is found, it may serve as a starting point for further inquiry into the possibility that one behavior results from the other. Policies and programs that aim to produce a desired outcome can be better targeted by understanding correlation and causality.

40 Define z-values

ANSWER In statistics, a z-value (also known as a standard score or standardized value) signifies the number of standard deviations that a data point or sample mean is above or below the population mean.

To calculate a z-value, you subtract the population mean from the data point or sample mean and then divide it by the population standard deviation or the standard error of the mean, respectively. The formula for calculating a z-value is:

$$z = (x - \mu) / \sigma$$

where z is the z-value, x is the data point or sample mean, μ is the population mean, and σ is the population standard deviation.

Z-values are important because they allow us to compare data points or sample means from different populations that may have different units of measurement or scales. By standardizing the values to a common scale, we can compare how far a data point or sample mean is from its respective population mean in terms of standard deviations.

41 Bring out the differences between Probability and Likelihood.

ANSWER According to the sample distribution of data, probability corresponds to determining the occurrence of some events, whereas likelihood refers to the probability of observing a particular set of data or evidence, given a specific hypothesis or model.

Consider a dataset containing the heights of students of class 10. The mean and the standard deviation of the data computed are 180 cm and 4.5 respectively.

When it comes to computing the probability of any scenario using this dataset, the characteristics of the dataset will remain unchanged. This means that the mean and standard deviation of the dataset will remain the same; they will not be changed in any way. Let us imagine we need to determine the chance that a random record in the dataset has a height of more than 180 centimeters; in that case, we will use the information provided below to make our determination.:
P (height > 180 cm | μ = **180, σ = 4.5**)

P (height > 180 cm | μ = 180, σ = 4.5)

For the same dataset, the probability of height > 180 cm has to be calculated, then in the above equation, only the height part would have changed.

Consider the exactly same dataset example, if their Likelihood of height > 180 cm has to be calculated, then it will be done using the information shown below:
Likelihood (μ = 180, σ = 4.5 | **height > 180cm**)

Likelihood (μ = 180, σ = 4.5 | height > 180cm)

In this section, the properties of the dataset will be changed, namely the mean and standard deviation of the dataset, to obtain the greatest likelihood for a height of more than 180 centimeters.

The term "probability" refers to the process of determining the likelihood that a certain event will occur, whereas the term "likelihood" refers to the process of increasing the likelihood that an event will occur.

42	**Define each of the following as classical, empirical, or subjective probability**
	a. The probability of drawing an Ace from a deck of cards
	b. The probability that I will finish writing this book before my deadline.
ANSWER	a. The probability of drawing an Ace from a deck of cards → **Classical Probability**
	b. The probability that I will finish writing this book before my deadline. → **Subjective Probability**
43	**What technique is better to go with mean vs median vs mode?**
ANSWER	• If the given dataset is a positively skewed distribution, then the first mode is used, the second median, and lastly mean is used.
	• If the given dataset is a negatively skewed distribution, then the first mean is used, the second median, and lastly mode is used.

CHAPTER 3

PROBABILITY AND HYPOTHESIS

1 **What is a Random Variable?**

ANSWER Random variable are the values that alter randomly, i.e., with no particular pattern. Random variables come in two varieties: discrete and continuous and discrete. For example, the quantity of defective goods made by a certain manufacturing plant for each batch, the marathon time of a runner, the weight of an animal like a dog.

2 **Define Probability.**

ANSWER Probability theory is the branch of mathematics that deals with numerical representations of the likelihood that an event will happen or that a proposition is true. The probability of an occurrence is a number between 0 and 1, with 0 denoting impossibility and roughly denoting certainty.

3   **List the properties of Probability**

ANSWER   The probability is the ratio of the chances of obtaining a desired output over all possible outputs. Always it lies between 0 and 1.

Probability values close to 1 indicate that an occurrence is probable, whereas probabilities close to 0 show that an event is not probable. Additionally, the probability values for all conceivable outcomes added together will equal 1.

4   **What is the formula for Probability?**

ANSWER   The possibility that one event will occur out of a group of potential outcomes of an experiment can be used to explain probability. It is calculated as number of favorable outcomes divided by total number of possible outcomes.

$$P(E) = \frac{\text{Number of favorable outcomes}}{\text{Total number of possible outcomes}}$$

5   **Define expected value.**

ANSWER   The expected value is the average result of a test that is repeated infinitely many times with various probabilities for each event. It is sometimes referred to as the weighted average. When a distribution is supplied, the mean of the distribution, or the average of the values, is used. It is computed as $\Sigma x * P(x)$.

Where x is the data value and P(x) is the probability of the value.

6   **What do you understand by Probability Distribution mean?**

ANSWER   In probability theory and statistics, a probability distribution is a mathematical function used to determine the likelihood of occurrence of a set of alternative events. It is a mathematical description of the relationship between a phenomenon's sample space and the events that may occur inside that region. Examples include weather forecasting, bowling average in cricket, flipping a coin, dice, lottery tickets, playing cards, etc.

7   **Explain the types of Probability Distribution?**

ANSWER   Probability Distributions may be split into two categories - Continuous and Discrete Probability Distribution.

8   **Explain continuous probability distribution.**

ANSWER   A continuous probability distribution is the probability distribution of a continuous variable. A Bell curve may be seen in the continuous probability distribution visualisation as shown in figure 3.1.

Features of continuous probability distribution
- A continuous variable may take on any value between its minimum ($-\infty$) and maximum ($+\infty$) values.
- The area under the Bell curve and the sum of all the probabilities will be equal to one.
- The range of the variables values is therefore covered by continuous probability distributions.

A continuous variable is said to have a probability of zero when the likelihood of it ever taking on any value is so remote that it may be considered infinitesimally insignificant. Nevertheless, there is a probability that is greater than zero that a value will be included within a certain range of values.

Figure 3.1:Bell Curve

9 List out some of Continuous Probability Distribution

ANSWER
- Beta distribution
- Cauchy distribution
- Students t Distribution
- Exponential distribution
- Gamma distribution
- Logistic distribution
- Weibull distribution
- Fishers F Distribution

10 Define Discrete Probability Distribution

ANSWER A discrete probability distribution is the term used to describe the probability distribution of a categorical or discrete variable. In discrete probability distributions, the probabilities of just the feasible values are considered in the calculation. To put it another way, a discrete probability distribution does not include any components that have a probability value of zero. The probability of a discrete probability distribution is equal to one when all of its potential values are added together.

Features of discrete probability distribution

- Discrete probability distributions are defined for variables that can only take on a finite number of values or a countably infinite sequence of values. These values are often integers.
- The sum of the probabilities assigned by the PMF to all possible values of the discrete random variable must equal 1. This ensures that all possible outcomes are accounted for.
- Discrete distributions uses a probability mass function (PMF).

11 **List out some of Discrete Probability Distribution**

ANSWER
- Discrete uniform distribution
- Poisson Distribution
- Bernoulli Distribution
- Binomial Distribution
- Hypergeometric Distribution
- The Negative Binomial Distribution
- The Geometric Distribution
- Multinomial Distribution

12 **What is Binomial Distribution?**

ANSWER   In probability theory and statistics, the binomial distribution is a discrete probability distribution that only has two potential results for an experiment: success or failure.

13. What is the formula for calculating the Binomial Distribution?

$$p(x|n,p) = \left(\frac{n!}{x!\,(n-x)!}\right) p^x \,(1-p)^{n-x}$$

ANSWER

p (x | n, p): The value of the binomial distribution function is the likelihood that an event will occur precisely x times for n discrete occurrences where the probability of each event is p.

P(x): probability that the selected event is obtained x times out of the total of n trails.

(1-p): probability that something other than the chosen event will occur in all the other trails.

n: is the number of experiments

x: number of successes

14. Suppose that 80% of all students in computer science and engineering are placed. Find the probability that precisely seven students will be placed in their final year if a sample of 10 new students is chosen in that year.

ANSWER

- Being placed in the final year or not (yes or no) are the only two mutually incompatible outcomes.
- The trail (students) have a set number, which is 10.
- For getting a job, there is a 0.8 percent chance of success.

Hence, n= 10, p = 0.80, q = 0.20, x = 7

$$p(x = 7 \,|n,p) = \left(\frac{10!}{7!\,(10-7)!}\right) 0.80^7 \,(1-0.80)^{10-7}$$

P(x=7) = 0.2013. When the likelihood of getting put in the final year is 80%, there is a 20.13% chance that precisely 7 out of 10 students will be.

15 Define Poisson Distribution

ANSWER In probability theory and statistics, the Poisson distribution is a discrete probability distribution that is used to express the probability that a given number of events will occur within a specified window of time or space, provided that these events occur at a known constant mean rate and regardless of the interval since the last event. This distribution is used to express the probability that a given number of events will occur within a specified window of time or space.

16 What is the formula for calculating the Poisson Distribution?

$$P(x \mid \lambda) = \frac{e^{-\lambda} \lambda^x}{x!}$$

ANSWER x: is a Poisson random variable
λ: is an average
e: is Euler's number which is roughly 2.72

17 If a person can read, on an average, 10 pages of a book in one hour. Calculate the probability that in the next hour, the person will read exactly 8 pages.

$$P(x = 8 \mid \lambda = 10) = \frac{e^{-10} \, 10^8}{8!} = 0.113$$

ANSWER The probability that the person will read 8 pages in one hour is 11.3%

18 Differentiate between Dependence and Independence.

ANSWER As in statistics and the study of stochastic processes, independence is a fundamental idea in probability theory. Informally speaking, two occurrences are independent, statistically independent, or stochastically independent if their occurrence has no bearing on either their chances or probability of occurring. The probability distribution of two random variables is said to be independent if neither is impacted by the realization of the other.

Dependence is a fundamental concept in probability theory. When the result of the first event affects the result of the second event, two events are said to be dependent.

19 Define Conditional Probability

ANSWER In probability theory, conditional probability is a measure of the probability that an event will occur, given that another event has already occurred (via assumption, supposition, statement, or evidence). Many disciplines of mathematics as well as insurance, economics, and politics all make use of conditional probability.

This particular approach is predicated on event B occurring in some way connected to event A. In this case, a conditional probability analysis of the occurrence of event B with respect to A is possible.

The expression "the probability of event A given event B" or "the probability of event A given that event B has occurred" is commonly denoted as $P(A|B)$, or sometimes $P_B(A)$, when event A is of interest and event B is known or assumed to have happened.

For Example!

Based on product marketing, automobile companies use conditional probability to predict the probability that they will sell out a certain model. The two possibilities that follow are already known.
- P(promotion) = 0.35
- P (sell out ∩ promotion) = 0.15

Given that a specific model is being promoted on that particular day, an automotive manufacturer may use the following numbers to determine the likelihood that they will run out of a certain model before the end of the day:

P (sell out | promotion) = P (sell out ∩ promotion) / P(promotion)

P (sell out | promotion) = 0.15 / 0.35

P (sell out | promotion) = 0.428

Given that a promotion is being conducted on that particular day, the likelihood that the vehicle firm will sell out of the model is 0.428, which is equivalent to 42.8%. If the automotive manufacturer is aware in advance that a promotion will be conducted, they will be able to raise their inventory in advance, which will lower the likelihood of selling out during the campaign.

20 Twenty percent of diners pick up their food from a favorite neighborhood eatery. Find the likelihood that a takeaway client will choose a Masala Dosa given that 7% of all customers order this dish and pick it.

ANSWER P (take-out) = 20 / 100 = 0.2

P (take-out and Masala Dosa) = 7/100 = 0.07

We need to calculate the *conditional probability* P(Masala Dosa | take-out)

P (Masala Dosa | take-out) = P (take-out and Masala Dosa) / P(take-out)

= 0.07 / 0.2 = 0.35

Hence, there is a 35% chance that a customer who orders take-out will order a Masala Dosa.

21 **What exactly is Bayes' Theorem?**

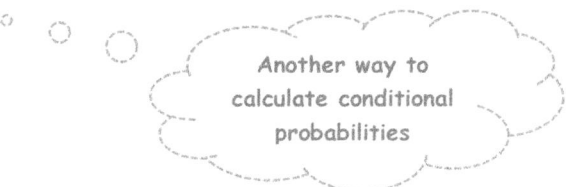

Another way to calculate conditional probabilities

ANSWER In probability theory and statistics, the Thomas Bayes-named Bayes' theorem (also known as Bayes' law or Bayes' rule) estimates the likelihood of an occurrence based on previously known factors that could be connected to the event.

22 Can you describe the Bayes' Theorem mathematical formula?

ANSWER The following equation is the mathematical formulation of Bayes' theorem.

$$P(A|B) = \frac{P(B \mid A)\, P(A)}{P(B)}$$

Where A and B are events and $P(B) \neq 0$
P (A | B) is the probability of event A occurring, given that event B has already occurred.
P (B | A) is the probability of event B occurring, given that event A has already occurred.
P (A) is the probability of event A occurring.
P(B) is the probability of event B occurring.

23 How to calculate conditional probabilities using Bayes' Theorem?

ANSWER The Bayes' Theorem can be used to determine the probability that an event will occur, given that another event has already happened. Given that we already know something about the circumstance, it is frequently used to determine the probability that something will occur. For instance, if a person tests positive for a disease, we may apply Bayes' Theorem to determine the probability that they actually have the disease.

24	**Why is Bayes' theorem important to data science education?**
ANSWER	Calculating conditional probabilities can be done using Bayes' theorem. Data scientists must frequently determine the probability of a certain event occurring given that another event has already occurred, hence Bayes' theorem is crucial.

25	**List out some real-world applications of Bayes' Theorem.**
ANSWER	Mathematics, medicine, economics, marketing, engineering, and many more all find uses for Bayes' Theorem.

26	**Before implementing the Bayes theorem, what crucial presumptions must be made?**
ANSWER	• Events are independent of each other • The outcomes of the events must have the same probability of occurring and that the event is fair

27	**Apply Bayes' Theorem in order to determine the likelihood that a brand-new television purchased at random is a Smart TV.**

	SmartTV	Plasma TV	Total
New	24	15	39
Used	9	12	21
Total	33	27	60

| ANSWER | Apply Baye's Theorem using the events A = SmartTV and B = new
$P(A \mid B) = P(A) P(B\mid A) / P(B)$
$P(\text{SmartTV} \mid \text{new}) = P(\text{SmartTV}) P(\text{new} \mid \text{SmartTV}) / P(\text{new})$
$= (33 / 60)(24/33) / (39/60)$
$= (0.55)(0.7273) / 0.65$
$P(\text{SmartTV} \mid \text{new}) = 0.615$ |

28 **Name the three properties that make up the normal probability distribution.**

ANSWER The normal probability distribution is a continuous distribution with a bell shape that satisfies the following three criteria:
- The mean, median, and mode all have the same value.
- The distribution is symmetric about the mean.
- The curve's entire area beneath the curve is one.

29 **Define Empirical rule.**

ANSWER According to the empirical rule of statistics, any piece of data with a normal distribution falls within three standard deviations of the mean. Additionally, called the 68-95-99.7 rule as shown in figure 3.2. According to the empirical rule, 99.7% of the data can be found within three standard deviations of the mean, 95% of the data can be found within two standard deviations of the mean, and 68% of the data can be found within one standard deviation of the mean.

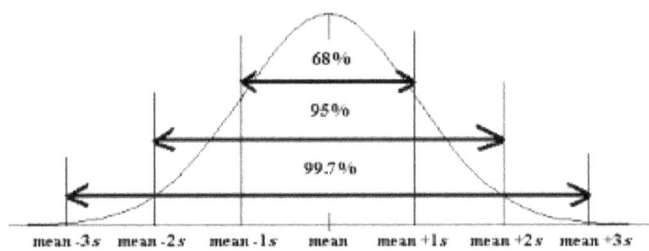

Figure 3.2: representation of empirical rule

30 **How much of a normally distributed data set lies within a standard deviation of the mean, one, two, and three, respectively, according to the empirical rule?**

ANSWER According to the empirical rule, 99.7% of the data can be found within three standard deviations of the mean, 95% of the data can be found within two standard deviations of the mean, and 68% of the data can be found within one standard deviation of the mean.

31 **How to determine the statistical importance of an insight?**

ANSWER To evaluate statistical significance, we need to do hypothesis testing. First, we begin by stating the null hypothesis and alternate hypothesis. Second, compute the p-value, which is the likelihood of getting the observed findings of a test if the null hypothesis is true. Finally, the level of significance (alpha) is determined, and if the p-value is smaller than the alpha, the null hypothesis is rejected – in other words, the result is statistically significant.

32. Discuss two-tailed hypothesis test. Outline the steps involved in two-tailed test.

ANSWER A two-tailed hypothesis test is used when the alternative hypothesis is presented as "not equal to," a specific value. In the above scenario, the alternative hypothesis states that the weight of the box containing mangoes is 18 kg. To have a better understanding of the two-tailed hypothesis test, consider the normal distribution curve that is shown below in figure 3.3.

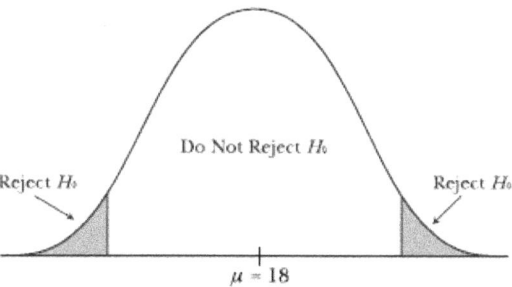

Figure 3.4: Representation of one-tailed hypothesis test

The distribution of samples for the typical weight of a box of mangoes is shown as a bell curve in the image. According to data, the population's average weight µ = 18 kgs. The mean of the sampling distribution is the null hypothesis. The level of relevance is indicated by the area of the darkened regions. The following steps below must be followed to do a two-tailed hypothesis test:

- Calculate the test statistic using the sample size of n; in this example, it is sample mean
- The sampling distribution curve should have the sample mean plotted on its x-axis.

- Do not reject H_0 if the sample mean falls inside the zone that is not colored; there is not enough data to support the alternative hypothesis, H_1.
- You have enough data to support the alternative hypothesis, H1, if the sample falls inside either of the shaded regions (also known as the rejection region).

This process is known as a two-tailed hypothesis test, since the preceding graphic contains two rejection zones.

33 Define one-tailed hypothesis test. Outline the steps involved in a one-tailed test.

ANSWER Whenever the alternative hypothesis is presented as "greater than" or "less than," a one-tailed hypothesis test is used. A firm that delivers groceries claims that its typical delivery time is under 15 minutes as shown in figure 3.4. The alternative hypothesis is that the issue will take 15 minutes, hence this problem statement has one tail. Look at the example below.

In this scenario, the shaded area on the left side of the distribution represents the rejection zone for a one-tailed test. The darkened region's area is determined by α. The following steps below must be followed to do a single-tailed hypothesis test:

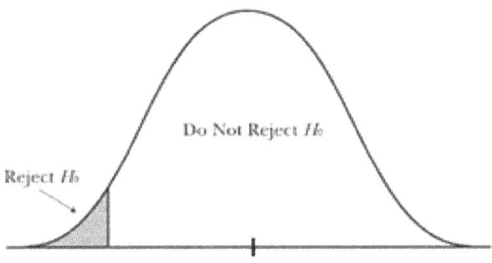

Figure 3.4: Representation of one-tailed hypothesis test

- Calculate the test statistic using the sample size of n; in this example, it is sample mean
- The sampling distribution curve should have the sample mean plotted on its x-axis.
- Do not reject H_0 if the sample mean is in the unshaded zone, you have insufficient data to support the alternative theory
- Reject H_0 if the sample mean is within the grey rejection region, there is sufficient evidence to support H_1

The business needs to just reject the null hypothesis in the delivery's instance time of groceries. The hypothesis (if the delivery time is 15 minutes or more) is rejected if the sample mean is sufficiently low to fall inside the shaded range.

34 **What do you understand by the term confidence interval?**

ANSWER A confidence interval (CI) is a range of estimations for an unknown parameter. When calculating a confidence interval, the degree of confidence that is used is important; the level of confidence that is most often used is 95%, although other levels, such as 90% or 99%, are also infrequently employed.

35 **Explain the differences between a mean point estimate and a confidence interval.**

ANSWER A point estimate for the mean is a mean derived from a sample that is then used to compute the mean of the population. A confidence interval is a range of values around a point estimate that most likely covers the mean of the actual population. This range is centred on the point estimate.

36 Defend the function of certainty levels in establishing a confidence interval.

ANSWER Confidence levels are used to express confidence intervals. Standard levels of confidence often fall between 90% and 98%. A 95% confidence interval is a range of values that surrounds the sample mean and has a 95% chance of including the actual population mean. As an example, this range of values is known as the sample mean. With two 95% confidence intervals, the smaller of the two is a closer approximation to the genuine population's mean.

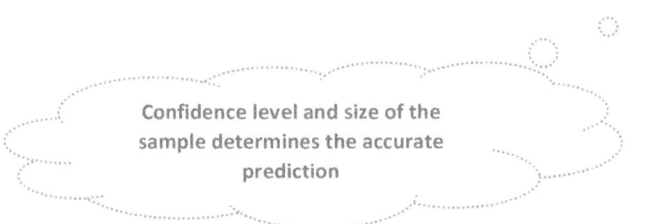

37 Explain p-hacking

ANSWER Data dredging, commonly referred to as data snooping, data dredging or p-hacking, is the misuse of data analysis to uncover patterns in data that can be presented as statistically significant, significantly raising the risk of false positives while understating it. The data are subjected to several statistical tests, and only the results of those that have significant findings are reported.

38 Explain the remedies for data dredging

ANSWER
- The best way to construct hypotheses while avoiding the practise of data dredging is to conduct randomised tests using data from outside the sample.

- The Bonferroni adjustment is another method for preventing data dredging. It involves keeping track of how many significance tests were performed during the investigation and dividing one's alpha standard for significance by this number.
- There is a clear distinction between confirmatory data analysis and exploratory data analysis when neither approach is applicable.
- In an effort to address very major problems like data dredging and HARKing, which have rendered theory-testing research very untrustworthy, academic publications are moving more and more towards the registered report format.

39 **Define A/B Testing or bucket testing or split-run testing**

ANSWER Two forms of a single variable, the control and the variation, are compared using A/B testing, a type of hypothesis testing that uses two samples. User experience and marketing are often improved and optimized using it.

40 **Explain the advantages and disadvantages of conducting A/B Testing.**

ANSWER

Advantages	Disadvantages
- The data can be quite helpful because it is based on actual user behavior, especially when deciding which of two solutions is superior.	- Depending on the size of the team and/or company, there can be a lot of meetings and debates on what precisely to test and what the A/B test's effect is.

• It also can offer solutions to highly particular design queries.	• It is highly time-consuming and expensive operation.
• Since it is directly comparing one thing to another, it is simple to determine what users like.	• A/B testing is beneficial for particular design challenges with clearly measurable results, but it can also have drawbacks because it is typically only beneficial for such situations.

41 Explain Bayesian Inference

ANSWER As new data or information becomes available, Bayesian inference uses the Bayes' theorem to update the probability of a hypothesis. In the dynamic examination of a sequence of data, Bayesian updating is especially crucial. Numerous fields, including science, engineering, philosophy, medicine, sports, and law, have used Bayesian inference. Subjective probability, often known as "Bayesian probability," and Bayesian inference, are closely connected concepts in decision theory philosophy.

42 Why Bayesian Inference Is Inconsistent?

ANSWER Bayesian inference has a number of weaknesses:
- Finding the prior probability is frequently difficult in most situations in the real world.

- MCMC (Markov chain Monte Carlo) sampling is employed when both the prior and likelihood become overly complicated. In actual situations, this moves rather slowly.
- The user may intentionally or unintentionally affect the outcome while quantifying prior knowledge.

CHAPTER 4

GRADIENT DESCENT

1 **What do you understand by Residual?**

ANSWER Residual is the differences between the Observed values and the values predicted by the model.

2 **Define Residual Sum of Squares (RSS)**

ANSWER In statistics, the residual sum of squares (RSS) is the sum of the squares of residuals. It is also known as the sum of squared residuals (SSR) and the sum of squared estimate of errors (SSE).

3 **Define Gradient Descent**

ANSWER Gradient Descent is an iterative approach that gradually moves in the direction of an ideal solution and is employed in a very wide range of circumstances as shown in figure 4.1.

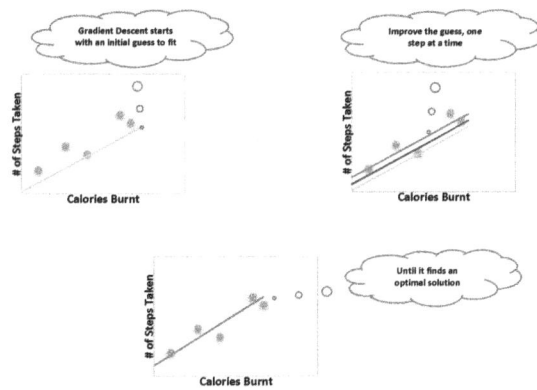

Figure 4.1: Working of Gradient Descent

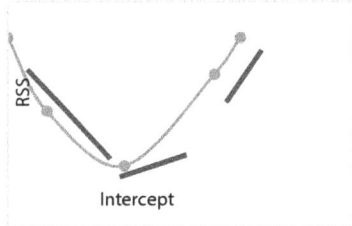

Started with the y-axis intercept=0, and then continue to get the lowest RSS. But how to know when do we need to stop?? This can be solved by taking the derivative of the curve. The derivative tells the slope of the tangent line that touches it.

In the above example, Gradient Descent fits a line step by step to these number of steps taken and Calories Burnt measurements. The Gradient Descent estimates the intercept and the slope of the line so that the Residual Sum of Squares (RSS) is minimized.

Regarding the graph located above, calculate the RSS for each point and the intercept and plot this curve that has RSS on the y-axis and the intercept on the x – axis.

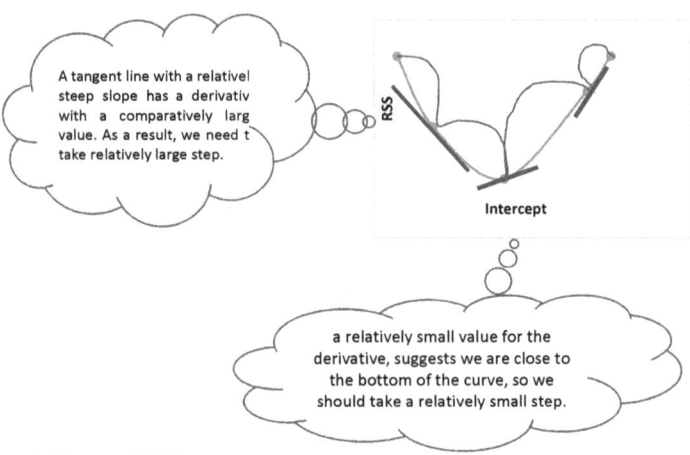

- A positive derivative indicates that we need to take a step to the left to get closer to the lowest RSS
- A negative derivative indicates that we need to take a step to the right to get closer to the lowest RSS

4 **Define Step Size.**

ANSWER The step size determines how quickly or slowly the method converges to a minimum and whether it diverges. Step size is calculated by the below given formula:

Step Size = slope * Learning Rate   or

Step Size = derivative * Learning Rate.

In machine learning and statistics, the Learning Rate adjusts step size at every step to reduce RSS. There are several methods for determining an appropriate beginning point for the learning rate. Starting with a huge value like 0.1, we may attempt exponentially smaller values like 0.01, 0.001, etc. to see which one gives us the best loss.

A decent step size makes rapid progress toward the minimum with each step. On the other hand, if the step size is too big, we could overshoot the local minimum repeatedly and never converge on it.

5 ANSWER

How to choose the right Step Size?

It takes more skill than science to determine the ideal step size. The following are common choices:
- Using a fixed step size
- The step size gradually getting smaller over time
- Selecting the step size at each step to reduce the value of the objective function

6 ANSWER

Outline the disadvantages of Gradient Descent and how can it be overcome

When there is a lot of data or multiple number of parameters, Gradient Descent slows down. This can be overcome by using Stochastic Gradient Descent.

7 ANSWER

Define Stochastic Gradient Descent

In stochastic gradient Descent, a random point from the dataset, is selected.

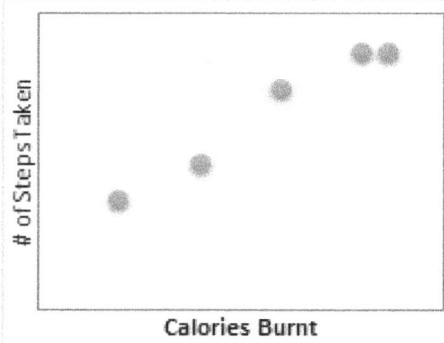

- Pick a random point from the dataset
- Evaluate the derivates at their current values
- Calculate the step sizes
- Calculate the new values
- Rather than selecting a single random point for per iteration, a subset of the observations can be selected.

8 Explain Mini-Batch Stochastic Gradient Descent.

ANSWER Rather than picking a single random point, a minor subsection of the data is randomly selected. This is known as the Mini-batch Stochastic Gradient.

By using a small subset, converges on the optimal values in fewer steps and takes much less time than using all the data.

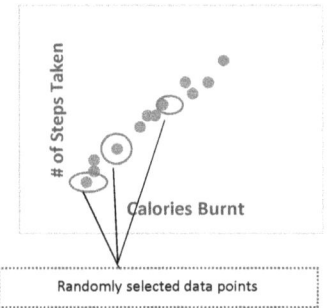

9 Differentiate between between Stochastic and Batch Gradient Descent

ANSWER

Batch Gradient descent	Stochastic Gradient Descent
Calculates the gradient using a subset of the training sample	Calculates the Gradient using single training sample

Slow and computationally expensive algorithm	Faster and less computationally expensive than Batch Gradient
Convergence is slow	Reaches the convergence much faster
Not recommended for large datasets	Can be used for large training sample

10 List some techniques for dealing with local minima problems.

Some of the methods that have historically been employed to address the issue of local minima include the following:
- judicious choice of features
- reliance on learning rate schedules
- Using various numbers of steps

11 Define local minima and global minima. How does local minima affect while calculating the gradient?

ANSWER

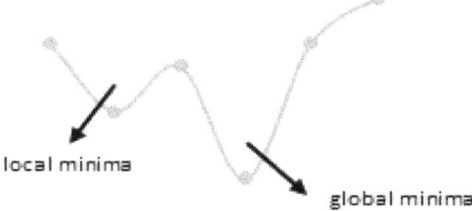

The location with the lowest value in a function's domain is known as the local minimum. By calculating the function's derivative, the local minimum can be calculated.

The function has another minimum value across the entire range, which is called the global minima.

It is possible to that we might get stuck at the bottom of the local minima instead of finding the way to the bottom and the global minimum.

CHAPTER 5

INTRODUCTION TO MACHINE LEARNING

1 Define model.

ANSWER A model is just a description of the relationship that exists between several variables mathematically (or probabilistically).

2 What do you understand by the term Machine Learning?

ANSWER Machine learning (ML) is a field of study that focuses on understanding and creating "learning" methods. These are the methods that use data to improve performance on a set of tasks. People think of it as a part of artificial intelligence. Machine learning algorithms use sample data, also called "training data," to make a model that they can use to make guesses or decisions without being told to do so.

Machine learning is used in a plethora of applications, such as

- Image and Speech Recognition
- Self-driving cars

- Virtual Personal Assistant
- Medical Diagnosis
- Automatic Language Translation
- Stock Market trading
- Product Recommendations

3 **How is Machine Learning used in day to day life?**

ANSWER Machine learning may help doctors make more accurate diagnoses. Chatbots with built-in voice recognition are being used by several clinicians to track patterns in patients' complaints. These personal assistants rely heavily on machine learning since they gather and improve the information based on your previous interactions with them. Alexa, for instance, is based on natural language processing, a method for converting utterances into words. Machine learning is also used in video surveillance, traffic prediction, Social Media Services, Search Engine result refining, online customer support, product prediction, etc.

4 **How is Machine Learning different from traditional application programming?**

ANSWER Traditional application programming encompasses computer processes that rely on manually crafted programs to process input data and generate outputs. In contrast, machine learning programming utilizes algorithms to analyze input data and automatically generate predictive models, thereby serving as a cornerstone technology in various augmented analytics applications. These predictive models enable forecasting future outcomes.

Unlike traditional programming, where rules are manually coded by humans, machine learning algorithms derive rules directly from data, resulting in increased potency and efficiency. This fundamental disparity distinguishes machine learning from traditional programming.

5   **Define Overfitting and Underfitting in Machine Learning.**

ANSWER   Overfitting is the process of creating a model that works admirably on the data you train it on but performs poorly on any subsequent data. This might involve discovering data noise.

Underfitting is the process of creating a model that does not function well even on training data; often when this occurs, you realize your model is inadequate and continue seeking for one that does.

6   **Explain why overfitting occurs and the ways to avoid overfitting**

ANSWER   Overfitting occurs when the model fits the training data very well and generalizes the new unseen data. Techniques to prevent overfitting are:
- Feature selection
- Data Augmentation
- Regularization
- Early stopping
- Cross validation and Ensemble
- Bagging and Boosting

7	**The trend of Machine Learning is rapidly developing. Explain it.**
ANSWER	Three primary reasons explain why machine learning is quickly expanding

- In recent years, we've been carrying smartphones in our pockets that boast computational capabilities nearly comparable to supercomputers of two to three decades ago. This surge in processing power facilitates rapid training of machine learning models.
- Because storage costs have gone down, it is now cheaper to store data, with machine learning. The algorithms autogenerate the rules from the data, making conventional programming less effective.
- Look at the innovations from the biggest research companies, like OpenAI or DeepMind, to see how much research has increased in the field of this Artificial Intelligence /Machine Learning in recent years.

8	**Explain the different types of Machine Learning algorithms.**
ANSWER	Three basic techniques are currently in use, namely: Supervised, Unsupervised and Reinforcement, while there are certain machine learning algorithm types that are only utilized in extremely particular use-cases as shown in figure 5.1.

Machine Learning Interview Questions

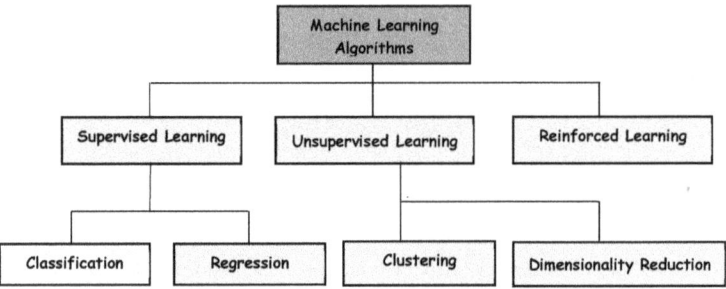

Figure 5.1: Classification of Machine Learning Algorithms

In supervised learning, machine learning models are trained using labelled data. The outcome in labelled data is already known. Mapping the inputs to the corresponding outputs is all that is required.

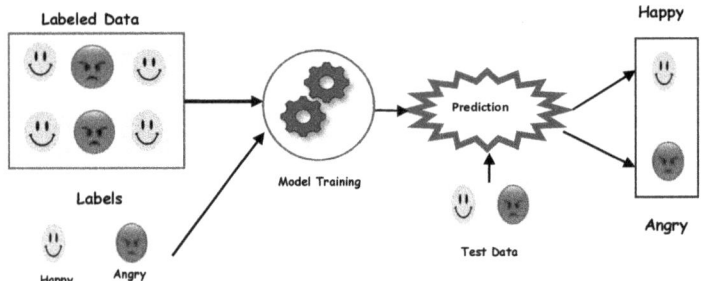

Figure 5.2: Working of Supervised learning

In this example, we have smiley images labelled with angry or happy as shown in figure 5.2. This known data is given into the machine, which evaluates and learns how to associate these images based on features such as shape, size, clarity, and so on. When a new image is supplied to the system without a label, the machine can now properly predict that it is a happy and angry using previous data.

Supervised learning can be further broken down into two categories.

- **Classification:** When a categorical output variable has two or more classes, classification is used. E.g. yes or no, male or female, disease or no disease, spam or not a spam.
- **Regression:** When the output variable has a real or continuous value, regression is used. In this instance, a change in one variable is associated with a change in another variable, indicating a relationship between two or more variables. E.g. weather forecasting, salary based on experience, market forecasting.

In Unsupervised Learning, the machine learns on its own using unlabeled data. In the unlabeled data, the machine looks for patterns and responds.

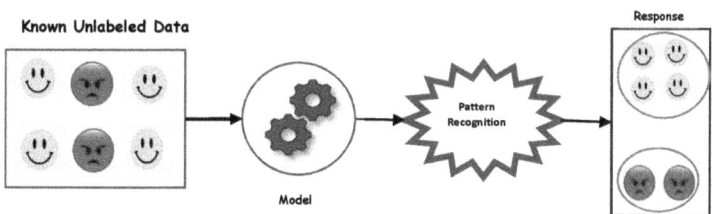

Figure 5.3: Working of unsupervised learning

Take the previous example as a starting point, but this time we will not specify to the machine whether it is an angry or happy smiley image as shown in figure 5.3. The computer separates the given set of patterns into two groups based on their patterns, similarities, etc.

Unsupervised learning can be further broken down into two categories.

- **Clustering:** The process of grouping objects into clusters that are distinct from one other and have similarities between them is known as clustering. E.g. Health insurance, Email marketing, Retail Marketing.
- **Dimensionality Reduction:** Dimension reduction / dimensionality reduction is the process of transforming data from a high-dimensional space to a low-dimensional space while maintaining the low-dimensional representation as close as feasible to the inherent dimension of the original data.

There is one more type included in Unsupervised learning called as Association. Finding the connections between variables in a huge database is done using an unsupervised learning technique called an association rule.

Reinforced Learning

Reinforcement learning (RL) is a subfield of machine learning that investigates how intelligent agents should operate in a given environment in order to maximize the concept of cumulative reward. Reinforcement learning, along with supervised and unsupervised learning, is one of the three fundamental machine learning paradigms.

In reinforcement learning, the objective is to identify a suitable action model which maximizes the agent's total cumulative reward. A general RL model's action-reward feedback loop is depicted in the figure 5.4 below.

Introduction to Machine Learning

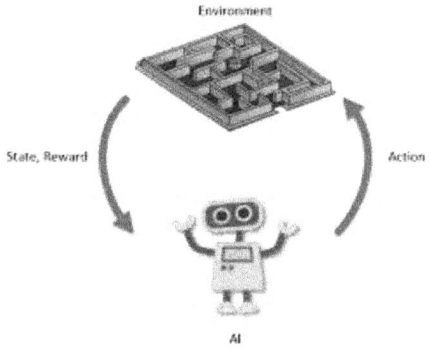

Figure 5.4: Working of reinforced learning

9. Discuss the pros and cons of Supervised Learning.

ANSWER

Pros of Supervised Learning

- Supervised learning in machine learning enables the capacity to collect data or generate data output based on past experience.
- Facilitates the application of experience to optimize performance criteria.
- Many practical computing problems may be solved with the help of supervised machine learning.

Cons of Supervised Learning

- The decision boundary may be overtrained if the training set that was employed did not include the kinds of examples you wanted in a class.
- Select several high-quality examples from each class to use when training the classifier.
- Big data classification may be difficult.
- The computing time required for training supervised learning is enormous.
- Unwanted Data decreases the efficiency
- Always in need of updates

10 — List out the advantages and disadvantages of Unsupervised Learning

ANSWER — **Advantages of Unsupervised Learning**

- Human minds cannot picture what Unsupervised Learn can see.
- It has many uses in real-time and is used to uncover hidden patterns that are of the utmost relevance to the industry.
- The results of an unsupervised task could lead to the start of a whole new business industry.
- The complexity is lower.
- Unlabeled data is slightly simpler to acquire.

Disadvantages of Unsupervised Learning

- It is costlier since comprehending the patterns and connecting them with domain expertise may need human involvement.
- Because there is no label or output measure to check the utility of the generated findings, it is not always assured that they will be beneficial.
- A task that is unsupervised makes it impossible to precisely describe the output and sorting. It strongly depends on the model, which in turn depends on the hardware.
- The results often have lesser accuracy.

11 **Outline the differences between supervised and unsupervised algorithm**

ANSWER

Supervised Learning	Unsupervised Learning
It uses known and labelled data as input	Unlabeled data are used as input.
It uses simpler method	It is computationally complex
Highly accurate	Less accurate compared to Supervised Learning
Direct feedback is considered by the Supervised Learning Model to verify whether the expected output is accurate.	No feedback will be accepted by the unsupervised learning model
The total number of classes is known	The number of classes is unknown
Algorithms Used are: • Linear and Logistic Regression • Support Vector Machine • Decision Tree and others	Algorithm Used are: • Hierarchical Clustering • Apriori Algorithm • K-Means Clustering and others
Some applications include spam detection, speech recognition, pattern recognition etc	Some applications include data processing, recommender systems, anomaly detection etc.

12 Describe classifier in Machine Learning

ANSWER Classification is the problem of identifying which of a set of categories (sub-populations) of an observation (or observations) belongs to. Classification is the problem of figuring out which of a set of groups (subpopulations) an observation (or observations) goes to. For example, putting an email in the "spam" or "non-spam" category or giving a patient a diagnosis based on things like their sex, blood pressure, the presence or lack of certain symptoms, etc.

Some of the classifiers used in machine Learning are Logistic Regression, Decision tree, Random Forest, Gradient boosted tree, Naïve Bayes, Support Vector Machine, K-Nearest Neighbor and others.

13 What is Confusion Matrix?

ANSWER A confusion matrix is a table that is often used to evaluate the performance of a classification model. It allows visualization of the performance of an algorithm by displaying the counts of true positive, true negative, false positive, and false negative results in a matrix format.

In a binary classification problem, the confusion matrix has two classes, often labelled as "positive" and "negative."

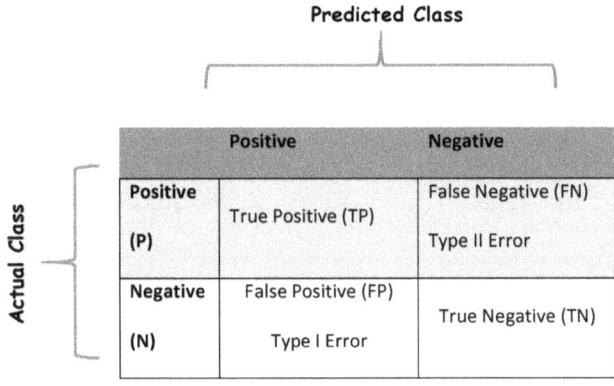

Where P is the total number of true positives and N is the total number of true negatives. Let us examine the four outputs of Confusion Matrix.

True Positive (TP): The cases where the model correctly predicts the positive class.

True Negative (TN): The cases where the model correctly predicts the negative class.

False Positive (FP): The cases where the model incorrectly predicts the positive class (Type I error).

False Negative (FN): The cases where the model incorrectly predicts the negative class (Type II error).

The confusion matrix helps in assessing the performance of a classifier and calculating various metrics such as accuracy, precision, recall, F1-score, and specificity. It provides a detailed breakdown of how well the classifier is performing and helps in understanding which classes are being confused with each other.

Sensitivity also known as Recall, True Positive Rate (TPR), hit rate. It trials how many positive cases the classifier has classified as positive. It should be higher.

$$Sensitivity = True\ Positive\ Rate = Hit\ Rate = Recall = \frac{TP}{TP+FN}$$

Specificity also known as True Negative Rate (TNR). It is a measurement of how many negative examples a classifier has classified as such. It should be high Specificity

$$Specificity = True\ Negative\ Rate = \frac{TN}{TN+FP}$$

Precision is the ratio of all positively classified cases that were accurately classified to all positively anticipated examples.

$$Precision = \frac{TP}{TP + FP}$$

The percentage of all forecasts that are accurate is known as accuracy.

$$Accuracy = \frac{TP + TN}{TP + TN + FP + FN}$$

The F1 score is a weighted average of recall and accuracy. When attempting to strike a compromise between precision and recall, the F1 score may be a useful option.

$$F1\ Score = 2 * \frac{Precision * Recall}{Precision + Recall}$$

14 What is the need for Confusion Matrix in Machine Learning?

ANSWER
- It determines the effectiveness of our classification model by evaluating how well classification models perform when they make predictions based on test data.
- Along with the classifiers' error, the error type—such as whether it is a type-I or type-II error—is also provided.
- To calculate the model's several parameters, including accuracy, precision, etc., use the confusion matrix.

15 List out some metrics to evaluate classification models.

ANSWER Depending on the classification model, the following are some of the evaluation metrics used.

1. Accuracy
2. Precision
3. Recall
4. F1 Score

16 Define Ensemble Learning

ANSWER By combining many learning algorithms, ensemble approaches in statistics and machine learning may improve expected performance beyond that of any single learning algorithm. There are three types of ensemble learning methods: bagging, stacking, and boosting.

Bagging: Bagging is the process of averaging the results of several decision trees that have been fitted to diverse samples of a single dataset.

Stacking: When several different model types are fitted to the same data, stacking is used to discover the best way to combine the predictions.

Boosting: Boosting involves adding ensemble members in a systematic way to correct the predictions made by previous models. The result is a weighted average of the forecasts.

17 Describe Dimensionality Reduction in Machine Learning.

ANSWER Dimension reduction or dimensionality reduction is the process of converting data from a high-dimensional space to a low-dimensional space with the aim of preserving the low-dimensional representation as near as possible to the inherent dimension of the original data.

Following are some advantages of using the dimensionality reduction technique on the provided dataset:

- The space required to store the dataset is lowered when the dimensions of the features are reduced.
- For features with fewer dimensions, less computation training time is needed.

- Rapid data visualization is made possible by the dataset's features with reduced dimensions.
- By addressing multicollinearity, it eliminates redundant features (if existent).

There may be some data lost due to Dimensionality Reduction and some of the principal components to be considered are unknown.

The several techniques for dimensionality reduction include:
- Principal component analysis (PCA)
- Linear Discriminant Analysis (LDA)
- Generalized Discriminant Analysis (GDA)

Principal Component Analysis (PCA)

PCA operates under the constraint that the variance of the data in the lower dimensions space should be as small as possible when the data in a higher dimensional space is mapped to data in the lower dimensional space. The steps involved in PCA are as follows:
- Create a data covariance matrix.
- Find this matrix's eigenvectors.
- In order to recover a significant portion of the variance of the original data, eigenvectors corresponding to the biggest eigenvalues are used.

There may have been some data loss as a result, and we are left with fewer eigenvectors. However, the remaining eigenvectors should hold on to the most significant variances.

Linear Discriminant Analysis (LDA)

Fisher invented Linear Discriminant Analysis (LDA), which is the most important and traditional method. Finding the category of a sample item with the closest mean by group or class is the goal of LDA. Every group has an approximate mean vector of the characteristics vectors of all the objects belonging to that category. The closeness is calculated by metric distance. It works well when the samples are normally multivariate and with equivalent covariance between different groups. LDA's drawbacks are the fact that multivariate normality is violated and that the LDF function value is often less than 0 or more than 1, which cannot be clarified.

Generalized Discriminant Analysis (GDA)

The kernel function operator is used in GDA to cope with nonlinear discriminant analysis. The input vectors are mapped using the GDA method into a high-dimensional feature space. The goal of GDA is to maximize the ratio of between-class scatters to within-class scatters in order to identify a projection for the features into a lower-dimensional space. The fundamental goal is to convert the input space into a useful feature space, where variables are related to the input space nonlinearly.

18 Discuss bias in data.

ANSWER Bias in data indicates that data is inconsistent. Multiple, mutually exclusive causes may account for the inconsistency. Generally speaking, a machine learning model examines the data, looks for patterns, and then makes predictions. These patterns are discovered by the model during training and are then used to make predictions using test data. Bias errors, or bias-related mistakes, refer to discrepancies between the predicted values of a model and the actual or expected values that occur during the prediction process.

A model has one of the following properties:

Low Bias: A model with low bias will make fewer assumptions regarding the nature of the target function.

High Bias: A model exhibiting high bias tends to rely heavily on assumptions, resulting in a diminished capacity to capture the essential characteristics of our data. Such a model is also unlikely to perform effectively when presented with new data.

19 Discuss variance

ANSWER The variance of a random variable quantifies the extent to which it deviates from the predicted value. A model should ideally not differ significantly from one training dataset to the next, showing that the method is effective in uncovering the hidden relationship between the input and output variables. The low variance and large variance are the 2 kinds of variance errors.

Low variance symbolizes a minor fluctuation in the target function's prediction as a result of alterations to the training data set. High variance displays a significant fluctuation in the target function prediction because of changes to the training dataset.

20 What is Data Leakage? Explain how to avoid data leakage.

ANSWER When data from sources other than the training dataset is used to build the model, this is known as "data leakage." As a result, the predicted performance of the mode being produced may be deemed inaccurate. This new information may enable the model to learn or know something that it otherwise would not know.

Methods to aid in preventing Data Leakage are

- Rectifying Duplicates and Understanding the Dataset
- Regarding Target Variable Correlation and Temporal Ordering, Feature Selection
- dividing the dataset into groups for training, validation, and testing
- After splitting, normalizing, but before cross-validation
- A Healthy Skepticism in Model Performance Evaluation

21 Define Cross Validation

ANSWER To test your model and select the hyperparameters, divide the entire training set into two subsets: training and validation set. This technique is known as cross-validation. In order to lessen the bias that would result from using just one validation set, you must repeat this process several times while choosing alternative training and validation sets.

22 Define Leave- One-Out Cross Validation

ANSWER The Leave-One-Out Cross-Validation, or LOOCV, procedure is used to assess machine learning algorithms when generating predictions on data that was not used to train the model.

Although it yields a trustworthy and objective measure of model performance, the process is computationally expensive to conduct. There are situations where the process should not be used, such as when you have a very large dataset or a computationally expensive model to evaluate, despite being straightforward to apply and requiring no configuration to be specified.

23 What is K-fold cross validation?

ANSWER Cross validation using the K fold method involves choosing a hyperparameter named k. The dataset has now been split into k pieces. We now use the first portion as the training set and the remaining k-1 as the validation set. The second part is then used as the validation set, while the remaining k-1 parts are used as the training set. It ought not to be applied to time series data.

24 How to choose the K value in cross validation?

ANSWER When choosing K, two factors must be considered: the quantity of models we receive and the size of the validation collection. We do not want there to be only two or three models. A less biased choice about the metrics is provided by at least 4 models. On the other hand, we prefer the dataset to account for at least 20–25 percent of the total data. in order to maintain a minimum ratio of 3:1 between the training set and the validation set.

It's good to use K as 4 for small datasets and K as 5 for large datasets.

25 **What do you mean by "feature selection," and what makes it essential?**

ANSWER The process of feature selection is used to choose the important features for the model to train on. To exclude the inappropriate features that cause the model to perform poorly, feature selection is necessary.

26 **What do you understand by Data Science?**

ANSWER In the branch of study known as "Data Science," enormous volumes of data are analysed using cutting-edge tools and methods in order to spot patterns and gain new understanding. The five stages of the data science life cycle are acquisition, maintenance, processing, analysis, and communication.

Data scientists must possess technical skills in statistics, linear algebra, and programming, as well as being able to use technical tools such as Apache Hadoop and Cloud computing. In addition to this, they need to have a strong understanding of business practises as well as strong analytic and organisational skills in order to formulate questions, gather information from a variety of sources, arrange it in a logical fashion, transform the outcomes into solutions, and communicate their findings.

Data science is an interdisciplinary field as depicted in figure 5.5

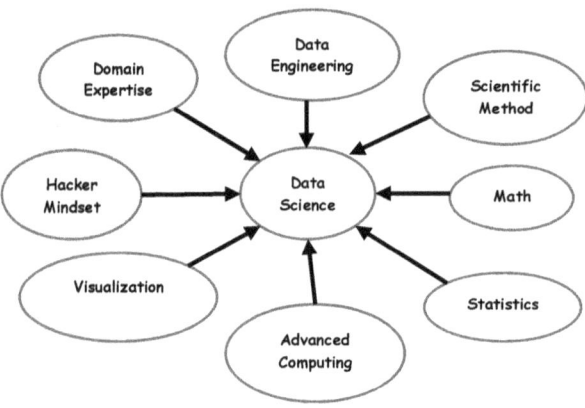

Figure 5.5: Data Science as an Interdisciplinary Field

27 **Define and explain the different types of Data Analytics.**

ANSWER   Data Analytics is the process of analyzing data to gain insights, identify trends, and make informed decisions. There are four main types of data analytics and they are Prescriptive, Diagnostic, Predictive, and Descriptive.

Descriptive analytics concentrates on what has occurred in the past, and is used to understand the data, summarize it, and develop insights from it.

Diagnostic analytics looks at why something has happened in the past, and can help identify and diagnose problems.

Predictive analytics uses data to make predictions about what might happen in the future. It can be used to predict customer behavior, detect patterns, and identify trends.

Finally, **prescriptive analytics** provides advice or recommendations on how to act in certain situations. It can help identify the best courses of action or strategies, and help business owners make informed decisions

28   **Explain the key distinctions between data science and data analytics.**

ANSWER   Data Science and Data Analytics are two distinct but related fields.

Data Science	Data Analytics
Data science aims to extract insights and knowledge from large and complex data sets through the use of advanced algorithms and machine learning techniques.	Data analytics focuses on the examination of data to identify trends and patterns.
Data science involves predictive modelling, data mining, and artificial intelligence	Data analytics is more focused on data visualization, descriptive statistics, and business intelligence
Data science is used to build predictive models and develop new products or services	Data analytics is often used to solve specific business problems

CHAPTER 6

K- NEAREST NEIGHBORS

1 **Explain the K-Nearest Neighbors Algorithm.**

ANSWER The K-Nearest Neighbor's algorithm (K-NN) is a non-parametric supervised learning method. It is used for classification and regression.

In K-Nearest Neighbor classification algorithm, works in a way that a new data point is assigned to a neighboring group to which it is most similar. K can be an integer larger than 1 in the K nearest neighbours. Therefore, we determine which nearby group each new piece of data is closest to in order to classify it.

Example: Imagine that we have a picture of a musical instrument that resembles both drum and guitar, but we are unsure if it is drum or guitar as shown in figure 6.1. Since the KNN algorithm relies on a similarity metric, it can be used for this identification. The KNN model will compare the new data set's features to those of drum and guitar images, and depending on which features are the most similar, it will classify the data as belonging to the drum or guitar.

Figure 6.1: Classification of the given object

The output of K-Nearest Neighbor regression algorithm is the object's property value. The average of the values of the K- closest neighbors makes up this number. K-NN can be used to forecast how a certain stock market will develop in the future.

2. Define similarity

ANSWER The similarity/feature similarity metric quantifies how similar two data items are. In a machine learning environment, a similarity measure is a distance with dimensions that represent the attributes of the objects. The similarities between the characteristics are greatest when the distance is minimal. While there will be little similarities if the distance is great.

The most popular similarity metric used are as follows:

- **Euclidean Distance:** Euclidean distance is the best proximity metric for dense or continuous data. The path's length serves as the Euclidean distance between any two places. This distance between two points is determined by the Pythagorean theorem.

- **Manhattan Distance:** The Manhattan distance is a measure that calculates the distance between two places as the sum of their absolute differences in Cartesian coordinates. If p1 and p2 are the data points in a plane with p1 at (x1, y1) and p2 at (x2, y2). The Manhattan distance is given by

    Manhattan distance = |x1 − x2| + |y1 − y2|

- **Minkowski Distance:** The Minkowski distance or Minkowski metric is a metric in a normed vector space which can be considered as a generalization of both the Euclidean distance and the Manhattan distance. If p1 and p2 are the data points in a plane with p1 at (x1, y1) and p2 at (x2, y2). If p is not specified, a default value of $p = 1$ will be used.

$$D = \left(\sum_{i=1}^{n} |x_i - y_i|^p \right)^{\frac{1}{p}}$$

- **Cosine Similarity:** The normalized dot product of the two attributes is determined by the cosine similarity measure. Given two vectors of attributes, A and B, the cosine similarity, $\cos(\theta)$, is represented using a dot product and magnitude as

$$Cosine\ Similarity = \cos \theta = \frac{A \cdot B}{\|A\|\|B\|} = \frac{\sum_{i=1}^{n} A_i B_i}{\sqrt{\sum_{i=1}^{n} A_i^2} \sqrt{\sum_{i=1}^{n} B_i^2}}$$

- **Jaccard Similarity:** The Jaccard index, also known as the Jaccard similarity coefficient, is a statistic used for gauging the similarity and diversity of sample sets.

$$J(A,B) = \frac{|A \cap B|}{|A \cup B|}$$

3. Can you provide real world instances where the K-NN algorithm might be useful?

ANSWER Classification, regression, and outlier identification are just a few of the tasks that may be accomplished with K-NN. Here are some particular examples:
- Classifying handwritten images
- Predicting the price of the shares based on features
- Finding genes relating to a certain disease

4. Explain the working of K-Nearest Neighbor

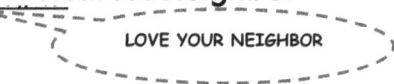

ANSWER The K-Nearest Neighbors (K-NN) method predicts the values of new datapoints based on "feature similarity," which further indicates that the new data point will be given a value depending on how closely it resembles the points in the training set. The steps below help to comprehend the working of K-NN algorithm.

I. A dataset is necessary before we can build any algorithm. We must therefore load both the training and test data at the first step of K-NN.

II. The second step is to choose the nearest data points, or K, based on the value. Any number, K, is possible.

III. Execute the actions listed below, one for each point in the test data.

a) Calculate the distance using either the Euclidean, Manhattan, or Hamming methods between each row of training data and the test data. Euclidean is the approach that is most frequently used to compute distance.

b) Sort them now in ascending order based on the distance value.

c) select the top K rows from the sorted array.

d) Depending on the most common class of these rows, it will give a class to the test point.

5. What should the ideal value of K be for the K-NN algorithm?

ANSWER
- The ideal value for "K" cannot be calculated in any particular way, so we must experiment with different values to see which one works best. K is usually set to the number 5.
- The model may experience the impacts of outliers if K is set to a very low number, such as K=1 or K=2.
- While K should have large values, there may be some challenges.

6. What is K-NN imputer?

ANSWER In statistics, imputation is the process of replacing missing data with substituted values. We can use K-NNImputer available in Scikit-Learn library to impute the missing values.

7. List out the advantages and disadvantages of K-Nearest Neighbor

ANSWER **Advantages of K-NN**

- Easy and simple algorithm to understand
- Applied to nonlinear data
- K-NN can be used to both classification and regression
- The procedure does not call for the creation of a model, the adjustment of various model parameters, or the formulation of new assumptions.

Disadvantages of K-NN

- Demand for large storage and does not scale well.
- K-NN is prone to overfitting and K-NN falls a victim of curse of dimensionality.
- Slow prediction rate
- When there are more cases, predictors, or independent variables, the algorithm gets slower.

8 Define curse of dimensionality. Why do we care about it?

ANSWER The term "curse of dimensionality" describes a number of phenomena that emerge when data is organized and analyzed in high-dimensional contexts but not in low-dimensional ones, like the three-dimensional physical realm of daily experience.

The points across that dimension are stretched when a new dimension is added, further separating them. High dimensional data are exceedingly sparse due to the increased spreading of the data caused by more dimensions. We are concerned about curse of dimensionality because sparse data makes machine learning challenging.

9 Outline some of the dimensionality reduction techniques

ANSWER
- Independent Component Analysis (ICA)
- Principal Component Analysis (PCA)
- Factor Analysis
- T- distributed Stochastic Neighbor Embedding (T-SNE)
- Linear Discriminant Analysis (LDA)
- Singular value Decomposition (SVD)

10   What is the difference between Gaussian Mixture (GM) Model and K-Means?

ANSWER   When comparing the two techniques, it appears that the Gaussian mixtures are more reliable. Because the EM (Expectation-Maximization) algorithm requires more iterations to attain convergence, GMs are typically slower than K-Means. They may also soon reach a local minimum, which is not the best course of action. The key challenges with K-Means clustering is an optimal number of clusters, the selection of the centroids, and the convergence rate.

11   Define K-Means clustering.

ANSWER   K-means is an unsupervised learning algorithm used for clustering problem. The goal of the vector quantization technique known as "K-Means clustering" is to divide a set of n observations into K groups, with each observation being assigned to the cluster that has the closest mean. K-Means clustering reduces variations within clusters. Within-cluster-variance is a straightforward indicator of compactness. In other words, the goal is to divide the data set into K divisions in the most compact way possible.

12   Describe the K-Means Clustering Algorithm's steps.

ANSWER   With K-Means clustering, n objects are divided into K clusters, and each object is assigned to the cluster that has the closest mean. This approach yields exactly K unique clusters with the highest level of distinction. It is necessary to compute the best number of clusters K that will result in the maximum separation (distance) because it is not known a priori. K-Means clustering aims to reduce the squared error function, or total intra-cluster variance:

$$J = \sum_{j=1}^{k} \sum_{i=1}^{n} \left\| x_i^{(j)} - c_j \right\|^2$$

Where J is objective function, k is the number of clusters, n is the number of cases, c is the centroid and is the distance function

K-Means Clustering Algorithm

a. Divide the data into K groups, where K is a predetermined number.
b. As cluster centers, choose K random sites.
c. Use the Euclidean distance function to assign items to the nearest cluster center.
d. Find the mean or centroid of each cluster of items.
e. Follow steps b, c, and d again to allocate the same points to each cluster in successive rounds.

13 **Mention some of the stopping criteria for K-Means clustering.**

ANSWER

a. In Convergence, the points remain in the same cluster with no further adjustments
b. The most iterations possible. The algorithm will finish after the allotted number of iterations has been reached. This is done in order to shorten the algorithm's runtime.
c. Variance did not decrease by x or more. The initial variance did not decrease by at least x times.

14 Compare K-Means and K-NN Algorithms

ANSWER A supervised learning approach is the foundation of the classification algorithm K-NN. An unsupervised learning approach is the foundation of the clustering algorithm known as K-Means clustering. For the K-NN algorithm, we need labelled data. Unlabeled points are required for K-Means clustering, which divides the points into groups based on their average distance from each other.

- The goal of the clustering method known as K-Means is to divide a set of points into K groups so that the points in each group tend to be close to one another. Because there is no external classification for the points, it is unsupervised.
- A classification algorithm known as K-Nearest Neighbors combines the classifications of the K closest points to a point in order to determine its classification (also known as regression). Because it attempts to categorize a point using the previously classified categories of other points, it is supervised.

15 List some of the applications of K-NN in Machine Learning

ANSWER
- Recommendation engines
- Finance
- Healthcare
- Pattern Recognition

16 **List out some disadvantages of K-Means clustering.**

ANSWER
- Data that comprises clusters of varying sizes and densities is difficult for K-Means to cluster.
- Centroids will be dragged by outliers, or the outliers may form their own cluster in place of being ignored. Prior to grouping, outliers should be clipped or eliminated.
- A distance-based similarity measure between any two samples converges to a constant value as the number of dimensions rises. Prior to clustering, lower the dimensions.

CHAPTER 7

NAÏVE BAYES

1. **Define Naïve Baye's Classifier.**

ANSWER The Nave Bayes algorithm is a supervised learning method for classification issues that is based on the Bayes theorem. In probability theory and statistics, Bayes' theorem (alternatively Bayes' law or Bayes' rule), named after Thomas Bayes, describes the probability of an event, based on prior knowledge of conditions that might be related to the event. Bayes' theorem is stated mathematically as the following equation

$$P(A|B) = \frac{P(B \mid A)\, P(A)}{P(B)}$$

Where A and B are events and $P(B) \neq 0$
- P (A | B) is the probability of event A occurring, given that event B has already occurred.
- P (B | A) is the probability of event B occurring, given that event A has already occurred.
- P (A) is the probability of event A occurring.
- P(B) is the probability of event B occurring.

2. Why is Naive Bayes known as Naive?

ANSWER Because of its extremely too optimistic assumptions—that all of the attributes in the dataset are equally significant and independent—which are rarely realized most real-world applications, it is referred to as naïve. All the predictors have an equal impact on the result and are independent.

3 List out advantages and disadvantages of Naïve Baye's classifier.

ANSWER **Advantages of Naïve Bayes' classifier**

- Nave Bayes is a fast and simple machine learning technique for predicting a class of datasets.
- Both binary and multi-class classifications can be done with it.
- When compared to other algorithms, it performs well in predictions for several classes
- For issues involving text classification, it is the most widely used option.

Disadvantages of Naïve Bayes classifier

- Naive Bayes cannot discover the relationship between features because it presumes that all features are either independent or unrelated.

4 Explain the types of Naïve Bayes Model.

ANSWER The following lists the three different Naïve Bayes models:

Gaussian: The Gaussian model presupposes that features have a normal distribution. This shows that the model believes that predictor values are samples from the Gaussian distribution if continuous values rather than discrete values are used.

Multinomial: When the data is distributed in multiple ways, the Multinomial Naive Bayes classifier is employed. It indicates the category a given document falls into, such as Sports, Politics, Education, etc., and is largely used to solve document classification issues. Word frequency is used by the classifier as a predictor.

Bernoulli: In contrast to the Multinomial classifier, the Bernoulli classifier uses independent Boolean values as predictor variables, such as determining whether or not a word is used in a document. For jobs involving document classification, this model is renowned.

5 Outline the steps involved in the implementation of Naïve Bayes' in Python.

ANSWER The steps used to implement the Naïve Bayes' algorithm in Python are as follows
- Preprocessing of the data
- Naïve Bayes fitting to the Training set
- Predicting the test result
- Test the result's correctness
- Visualizing the test set result.

6 What is the best way to apply the Naive Bayes classifier on categorical features? Imagine if some characteristics were numerical.

ANSWER In a Naïve Bayes classifier, any predictor can be used. The conditional probability of a feature given the class P (F | Class) is required.
- The probability of P (F | Class) can be calculated for the categorical characteristics using a multinomial or Bernoulli distribution.

- The P (F | Class) for the numerical features can be calculated using a normal or Gaussian distribution.
- It is possible to substitute the specific distribution for a numerical feature that follows a different specific distribution, such as an exponential.
- A kernel density estimator can be used to estimate the probability distribution for numerical or categorical data that lacks a clearly defined distribution.

Naive Bayes can combine several types of features because it presumes the conditional independence of the features. To get the final prediction, we can compute the conditional probabilities for each characteristic and multiply them.

7 **Is it possible to select a classifier based on the size of the training set?**

ANSWER
- We can use algorithms with high bias/low variance like Nave Bayes and Linear SVM if the availability of data is a constraint, i.e. if the training data is smaller or if the dataset has fewer observations and a higher number of features.
- K-Nearest Neighbors, Decision trees, Random forests, and kernel SVM are examples of low bias/high variance methods that may be used if the training data is sufficiently big and the number of observations is more than the number of features.

CHAPTER 8

REGRESSION

1 Define Regression

ANSWER Regression is a statistical technique used to model the relationship between one or more independent variables and a dependent variable. It aims to predict the value of the dependent variable based on the values of the independent variables. This predictive modelling technique is commonly used for forecasting, hypothesis testing, and understanding the relationship between variables in various fields such as economics, finance, and social sciences.

2 List out the types of regression

ANSWER **Some of the types of regression are:**

- Linear Regression
- Polynomial Regression
- Logistic Regression
- Quantile Regression
- Ridge Regression
- Lasso Regression
- Elastic Net Regression
- Principal Component Regression
- Partial least Regression

- Support Vector Regression
- Ordinal Regression
- Poisson Regression
- Negative Binomial Regression
- Quasi Poisson Regression
- Cox Regression
- Tobit Regression

3 Differentiate between Classification and Regression

ANSWER

Classification	Regression
Classification is used to predict discrete values, such as an email being spam or not.	Regression predicts continuous values, such as stock prices.
In Classification, the goal is to accurately classify data points into predefined classes or labels.	Regression the goal is to predict a real-valued output.
Classification problems can be further divided into binary or multi-class classification.	Regression techniques can be divided into linear or non-linear.
Classification algorithms tend to be simpler to build.	Regression models are more complex.
Classification algorithms are used for predicting categorical data.	Regression algorithms are used for predicting continuous data.

4 When will you use Classification over Regression?

ANSWER Classification is used when the output is divided into distinct classes; it is the process of assigning a class label to an instance. Regression is used when the output is continuous; it is the process of producing a numerical estimate of a given quantity. Generally, classification is used when the goal is to predict a categorical output, while regression is used when the goal is to predict a numerical output.

5 List out some of the mathematical functions or best fit lines used in analytical models.

ANSWER Common types of mathematical functions used in analytical models are as follows

- **Linear function:** $y = a + bx$. Linear functions show steady increases or decreases over the range of x. This is the simplest type of function used in predictive models. It is easy to understand and, over small ranges of values, can approximate behavior rather well.
- **Logarithmic function:** $y = \ln(x)$. Logarithmic functions are used when the rate of change in a variable increase or decreases quickly and then levels out, such as with diminishing returns to scale. Logarithmic functions find application in marketing models, where consistent percentage increments in advertising yield consistent, absolute sales growth.
- **Polynomial function:** $y = ax^2 + bx + c$ (second order polynomial function), $y = ax^3 + bx^2 + cx + d$ (third order), and so on. A second order is parabolic in nature and has only one hill or valley; a third order polynomial has one or two hills or valleys. Revenue models that incorporate price elasticity are often polynomial functions

- **Power function:** $y = ax^b$. Power function defines phenomena that increase at a specific rate. Learning curves that express improving times in performing a task are often modelled with power functions having a > 0 and b < 0.
- **Exponential function:** $y = ab^x$. Exponential functions have the property that as x increases the value of y grows exponentially, with the rate of growth determined by the value of the base b. For example, the perceived brightness of a light bulb grows at a decreasing rate as the wattage increases. In this case, a would be *a* positive number and *b* would be between 0 and 1. The exponential function is often defined as $y = ae^x$ where b = e, the base of natural logarithms.

6 What is Multicollinearity?

ANSWER Multicollinearity is a phenomenon in which two or more independent variables in a multiple regression model are highly correlated with each other. This can lead to non-identifiable parameters, and is a characteristic of the design matrix, not the underlying statistical model. Multicollinearity is a problem that can adversely affect regression results, as it can create redundant information and skew the results in a regression model.

To detect multicollinearity, you can calculate correlation coefficients for all pairs of predictor variables. If the correlation coefficient is close to or exactly -1 or +1, one of the variables should be removed from the model if at all possible. Data-based multicollinearity is caused by poorly designed experiments, data that is 100% observational, or data collection methods that cannot be manipulated. Structural multicollinearity is caused by the researcher creating new predictor variables.

7 Describe the working of Linear Regression

ANSWER Linear Regression is a supervised machine learning algorithm used to predict numerical values. It examines linear relationships between variables, such as the relationship between inputs and outputs. Linear Regression tries to find the best fit line to the data points, which is determined by the coefficients of the equation that best fit the data points. This equation can then predict outcomes on new, unseen data.

The algorithm is used to predict the value of a dependent variable based on one or more independent variables. This can understand how changes in the independent variables affect the dependent variable. Linear Regression is the gateway to a general technique called Linear Models, which can create and evaluate models that go way beyond fitting simple lines to data.

8 Explain the types of Linear Regression

ANSWER Two different types of linear regression models exist.

Simple Linear Regression: One independent and one dependent variable makes up a simple linear regression model.

Multiple Linear Regression: A linear regression model with more than one independent variable and one dependent variable is known as multiple linear regression.

9 **What are the assumptions of Linear Regression?**

ANSWER Linear regression assumes that there is a linear relationship between the predictor variables and the response variable. It also assumes that the residual errors are independent and have a constant variance. Furthermore, it assumes that the predictor variables are independent of each other, which is referred to as the "no multicollinearity" assumption. Finally, it assumes that the residual errors are normally distributed. The variability of the errors should be the same across all values of the predictor variables. This can be tested using a residual plot.

10 **List out the disadvantages of Linear Regression.**

ANSWER Linear regression, while a versatile and useful tool, does have some drawbacks.
- The most notable is that it can only model linear relationships, meaning it cannot accurately represent the relationships between variables when they are non-linear. In those cases, more advanced models such as logistic regression are needed.
- Linear regression is sensitive to outliers, so any data points that are far from the average can significantly impact the results of the analysis.
- Linear regression assumes a linear relationship between the independent and dependent variables, which may not be true in all situations.

11 Define Logistic Regression. Explain the working of Logistic Regression

ANSWER Logistic Regression is a classification algorithm used to assign binary outcomes - either 0 or 1 - to input data. It is built upon a linear regression model, but instead of predicting a continuous value, the output is converted into a probability of belonging to one of two classes.

The working of Logistic Regression involves using an equation to represent the relationship between input and output variables. This equation can predict the probability of the output belonging to a particular class. The equation includes an intercept and coefficients for each input variable, which are estimated using a suitable optimization technique.

Once the coefficients are estimated, the equation can make predictions for new data. The prediction is based on a threshold which is determined by the user. Values below the threshold are assigned to one class and values above the threshold are assigned to the other class.

12 Explain the types of Logistic Regression.

ANSWER The types of Logistic Regression are as given below
- **Binary Logistic Regression:** Binary logistic regression classifies the object as yes or no solution. There are just two possible outcome answers. This concept is typically represented as a 0 or a 1 in coding. Examples include:
  o Whether or not to lend to a bank customer (outcomes are yes or no).
  o Assessing cancer risk (outcomes are high or low).
  o Will a team win tomorrow's game (outcomes are yes or no)

- **Multinomial Logistic Regression:** Multinomial logistic regression is a model where there are multiple classes that an item can be classified as. There is a set of three or more predefined classes set up prior to running the model. Examples include:
    - Classifying texts into what language they come from.
    - Predicting whether a student will go to college, trade school or into the workforce.
    - Does your cat prefer wet food, dry food or human food?
- **Ordinal Logistic Regression:** Ordinal logistic regression is also a model where there are multiple classes that an item can be classified as; however, in this case, an ordering of classes is required. Classes do not need to be proportionate. The distance between each class can vary. Examples include:
    - Ranking restaurants on a scale of 0 to 5 stars.
    - Predicting the podium results of an Olympic event.
    - Assessing a choice of candidates, specifically in places that institute ranked-choice voting.

13 **What is Sigmoid function in Logistic Regression?**

ANSWER Sigmoid function, also known as the logistic function, is a popular activation function used in a logistic regression model.

The sigmoid function is used to transform the linear output from a linear model into a non-linear output. It works by squashing the input values into the range (0, 1). Values above or below this range will be mapped to 0 or 1, respectively.

Mathematically, the sigmoid function is defined as $f(x) = \frac{1}{(1+e^{-x})}$. It takes in any real-valued number and returns a number between 0 and 1. Thus, the output of the sigmoid function can be interpreted as a probability.

The sigmoid function is a smooth and differentiable function, making it suitable for training neural networks. It is also used in probabilistic models, such as a logistic regression, where it estimates the probability of an event occurring.

14 When do we use Logistic Regression?

ANSWER Logistic regression is a machine learning algorithm used for classification problems.

- It is used when the output is a binary variable which can take only two values - 0 or 1.
- It is used to predict the probability of a categorical dependent variable based on one or more predictor variables.
- Logistic regression estimates the probability of the occurrence of a particular event by fitting data to a logistic function.
- It is widely used in applications such as predicting the risk of a disease based on symptoms, predicting the likelihood of a customer buying a product, and more.

15 **List out the disadvantages of Logistic Regression**

ANSWER Logistic regression has some disadvantages that need to be considered when using this model.
- It assumes that the data is linearly separable and that the relationship between the predictor variables and the response variable is logistic (i.e., follows an S-shaped curve). If this is not the case, then the model will not be able to accurately capture the relationship between the variables, leading to inaccurate results.
- It is sensitive to outliers; a single outlier can significantly affect the results.
- Logistic regression does not perform well when the classes are highly imbalanced (i.e., when one class has significantly more data points than the other).
- It can be computationally expensive to train, especially when there are a large number of predictor variables.
- Finally, logistic regression can be prone to overfitting, meaning that the model has learned the training data too well and is not able to generalize to unseen data.

16 **What are the key differences between Logistic Regression and Linear Regression?**

ANSWER Logistic regression and linear regression are two different types of machine learning algorithms that are used for different purposes.

Logistic regression is used for classification tasks, where it is necessary to classify data points into two or more discrete categories. This type of regression considers the relationship between one or more independent variables and a categorical dependent variable. The goal of logistic regression is to accurately predict the probability of an event (e.g. whether or not a customer will purchase a product) based on the values of the independent variables.

Linear regression, on the other hand, is used to predict a continuous target variable. This type of regression considers the relationship between one or more independent variables and a continuous dependent variable. The goal of linear regression is to accurately predict the value of the dependent variable based on the values of the independent variables.

In general, logistic regression is more suitable for classification tasks, while linear regression is more suitable for prediction tasks.

17   **Discuss Lasso Regression.**

ANSWER   Lasso regression is a type of linear regression technique that uses a "lasso" or a regularization parameter to reduce the complexity of the model by restricting the number of variables that can be used. The regularization parameter (lambda) is used to penalize the absolute size of the coefficients, reducing their numbers and forcing them to zero. This technique is used to prevent overfitting and to ensure that the model is well-conditioned and can generalize. It is also used to identify variables that are valuable predictors of the outcome.

18   **Explain the working of Lasso Regression.**

ANSWER   Lasso Regression is a type of regularized regression technique used when there are a large number of features from which to choose. It uses a penalty term, often referred to as the L1 norm, to reduce the complexity of the model and to select only a subset of the most relevant features for making predictions.

The L1 norm is calculated by summing the absolute value of the coefficients for each feature, with larger coefficients resulting in a higher penalty. This means that the L1 norm will select only the most important features and reduce the impact of less important features. This helps to reduce overfitting and can lead to more accurate models.

19 **List out the disadvantage of Lasso Regression**

ANSWER Here are some of the disadvantages associated with Lasso Regression.
- The most significant disadvantage is that Lasso Regression may not be as effective at fitting data that is highly correlated.
- Furthermore, it can be difficult to choose the optimal regularization strength parameter, as selecting too small of a value can lead to overfitting, while selecting too large of a value can lead to underfitting.
- Finally, Lasso Regression can be slow to fit compared to other techniques.

20 **Define Ridge Regression**

ANSWER Ridge Regression is a type of linear regression used to minimize overfitting caused by large numbers of features. It is used when there are too many features in a dataset, compared to the number of observations. This is also known as the problem of multicollinearity.

Ridge Regression adds a penalty to the least squares loss function which shrinks the coefficients of the model towards zero. This helps to reduce the variance of the predictions and creates a model that is less sensitive to the random fluctuation in the training data. By reducing the variance, the model generalizes better and is less likely to overfit the training data.

21 **Explain the working of Ridge Regression.**

ANSWER Ridge Regression is a type of regularized linear regression technique that is used to reduce the effects of multicollinearity (correlated predictors) in a regression model. It is also used to address overfitting in a dataset. It is a type of shrinkage model whereby a non-zero coefficient is set for all the independent variables. This will reduce the magnitude of the regression coefficients and make them more interpretable.

22 **List out the disadvantages of Ridge Regression**

ANSWER The main disadvantage of Ridge Regression is:
- It does not perform well when data is sparse (there are a lot of zeros in the dataset) and when the dataset has highly correlated predictors.
- Ridge Regression does not provide a feature selection mechanism, as all of the predictors are kept in the model.
- The interpretation of the coefficients is difficult as they are all shrunken towards zero.

23 **Bring out the key differences between Lasso Regression and Ridge Regression**

ANSWER Lasso and Ridge regression are two popular linear regression models that are used when working with small datasets. Both models have a regularization component that helps to reduce the variance in the model and avoid overfitting.

Lasso regression (Least Absolute Shrinkage and Selection Operator) adds an additional penalty term to the cost function that is the sum of the absolute values of the model coefficients. This penalty term helps to reduce the complexity of the model by shrinking some of the model coefficients to zero, thus reducing the number of features used in the model.

Ridge regression (also known as Tikhonov regularization) adds a penalty term to the cost function, that is the sum of the squares of the model coefficients. This penalty term helps to reduce the variance in the model and avoid overfitting.

Both Lasso and Ridge regression can provide better predictions than linear regression, but they also require more analysis to determine which model is best suited for the data. In general, Lasso regression is useful when there are a few underlying features that are important for the prediction and the data has a large number of noise features. Ridge regression is useful when there are many underlying features that are important for the prediction, and the data has a small number of noise features.

24 What is Regularization?

ANSWER Techniques that delay the onset of overfitting are called regularization. The two popularly used regularization methods are dropout and batchnorm.

25 Differentiate between L1 Regularization and. L2 Regularization.

ANSWER When it comes to regularization, there are two main approaches: L1 Regularization and L2 Regularization. These approaches are used to reduce the complexity of a model and prevent it from overfitting the data.

L1 Regularization, also known as the Lasso regularization, adds a penalty term to the cost function proportional to the sum of the absolute values of the weights. This encourages the model to use only the most important features and reduce the model's complexity.

On the other hand, L2 Regularization, also known as the Ridge regularization, adds a penalty term to the cost function proportional to the sum of the square of the weights. This encourages the model to use all the features, but to keep them small.

26 Explain advantages and disadvantages of L1 and L2 Regularization

ANSWER Both L1 and L2 regularization have their advantages and disadvantages. L1 regularization can reduce the complexity of a model, but it can also lead to underfitting. On the other hand, L2 regularization can force the model to use all the features, but can also lead to overfitting. Ultimately, which regularization approach to use depends on the specific problem and data.

27 When does Regularization become necessary in Machine Learning?

ANSWER Regularization is an important concept in machine learning and is essential to achieve good model performances. Regularization helps prevent overfitting, a common problem in machine learning where models are trained on a limited set of data and perform poorly on unseen data. Regularization works by introducing a penalty term that helps the model to 'learn' the underlying patterns in the data by introducing certain constraints or preventing certain coefficients or parameters from becoming too large. Regularization techniques are generally used when the model is prone to overfitting, such as with linear regression and logistic regression. Regularization helps to simplify models, reduce variance, and improve generalization.

28   **What is the effect on the coefficients of logistic regression if two predictors are highly correlated?**

ANSWER   When two predictors are highly correlated, the coefficients of logistic regression can become unstable and unreliable. This is because the coefficients of logistic regression depend on the variance of the data. If two predictors are highly correlated, they will have similar variances and thus, the coefficients will become unstable and unpredictable. To avoid this, it is important to analyze the data and select only uncorrelated predictors for logistic regression.

29   **How can you assess a good logistic model?**

ANSWER   Assessing a good logistic model requires evaluating several performance metrics, such as accuracy, precision, recall, specificity, and AUC or area under the curve. Additionally, it is important to compare the results of the model to a baseline to determine how much better the model is. Further, some methods, such as decision trees, K-nearest neighbors, or other ensemble can compare the performance of logistic regression models to other methods. Finally, cross-validation and hyperparameter tuning should be used to properly optimize the model.

CHAPTER 9

DECISION TREES

1 **Define decision tree. Explain the working of decision tree**

ANSWER Decision trees are a type of predictive model that are used to classify data into different categories. A decision tree is a tree-like graph of decisions and their possible consequences, including chance events, resource costs, and utility. Each node of the tree represents a "test" on an attribute (e.g. whether a coin flip comes up heads or tails), each branch represents the outcome of the test and each leaf node represents a class label (decision taken after computing all attributes). The topmost node in a tree is the root node as shown in figure 9.1.

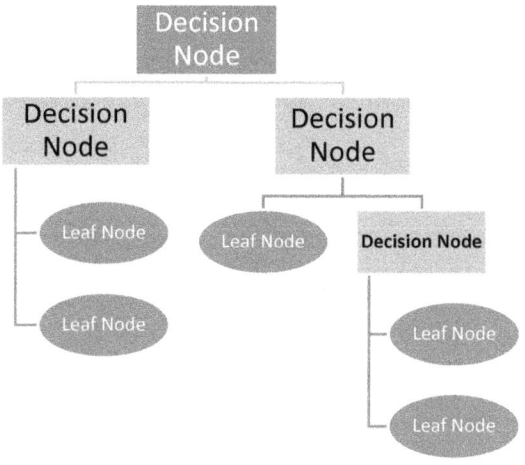

Figure 9.1: Representation of Decision tree

To build a decision tree, you start with a root node, where all the data is present. The root node is then split based on best attribute and each branch becomes a child node of the parent node. This process is repeated until the nodes reach the leaf nodes, which contain class labels. To determine which attribute to split on, the algorithm calculates the information gain of each attribute. Information gain is the reduction in entropy. Entropy is a measure of how much uncertainty there is in the data; the higher the entropy, the more mixed up the data is.

The decision tree is a powerful tool that is used in numerous areas of data science, from supervised learning to classification and regression. It is particularly useful for understanding the complex relationships between inputs and outputs, and for making predictions about the future.

2 Describe Overfitting trees

ANSWER Overfitting trees are a type of decision tree that is trained using too many features from a training dataset, and as a result, it is overly complex and does not generalize well when presented with unseen data. Overfitting trees tend to perform well on the training dataset, but do not perform well on the testing dataset because of poor generalization. This makes it difficult to draw reliable conclusions from the model. To prevent overfitting, one should use a simple decision tree with fewer features and hyperparameter tuning.

3 Explain splitting nodes in decision trees

ANSWER Splitting nodes is the process of deciding which feature of the data should be used to split the dataset into two subsets. The algorithm chooses the feature and value for the split that provides the most information gain, i.e. the resulting split gives the greatest homogeneity within each subset of data. The chosen split is then used to create child nodes which further divide the dataset until it is completely classified.

4 List a few well-known decision-tree-generation algorithms along with the criteria used to pick the attributes they utilize.

ANSWER Popular algorithms for creating decision trees include the following:

1. The ID3 (Iterative Dichotomiser) uses information gain as a criterion for choosing attributes.
2. C4.5 (the ID3 successor): Uses the Gain Ratio as an attribute selection criterion.
3. The CART (Classification and Regression Trees) algorithm uses the Gini Index as an attribute selection criterion.

5 **Enumerate the attribute selection criteria employed by the ID3 algorithm for constructing a Decision Tree.**

ANSWER The ID3 algorithm uses three attribute selection measures to construct a Decision Tree:

Information Gain: This measure determines how much information a given attribute can provide about the decision class. It calculates the expected reduction in entropy by splitting the set of records on the basis of a given attribute. Information Gain is calculated using the formula

$$IG(T,a) = H(T) - H(T|a)$$

Where T is a random variable and $H(T|a)$ is the entropy of T given the value of attribute a.

Gain Ratio: This measure corrects the Information Gain measure and helps to avoid attributes that split the dataset into many small subsets. It adds a new component to Information Gain, i.e. the intrinsic information, which is the ratio of number of subsets created and their sizes.

$$IGR(T,a) = \frac{-\sum_{i=1}^{n} P(T)\log P(T) - (-\sum_{i=1}^{n} P(T|a)\log P(T|a))}{-\sum_{i=1}^{n} \frac{N(t_i)}{N(t)} * \log_2 \frac{N(t_i)}{N(t)}}$$

Gini Index: This measure is used to calculate the impurity of a node. It is the probability of misclassifying a randomly chosen sample. It is calculated by subtracting the sum of the squares of probability of each of the class from 1. The formula for calculating Gini index

$$Gini = 1 - \sum_{i=1}^{j} P(i)^2$$

6 Explain the CART Algorithm for Decision Trees.

ANSWER The CART (Classification and Regression Trees) Algorithm is a supervised learning model used for classification and regression problems. It is a popular algorithm and is used in many different applications such as finance, medicine, and engineering.

The CART algorithm works by generating a decision tree from a given dataset. The algorithm first splits the dataset into subsets, then assigns a decision node to each subset, and finally assigns a terminal node (leaf node) to each subset. The algorithm then evaluates each decision node by measuring the quality of the split and assigns a terminal node (leaf node) to the final split.

The CART algorithm is a recursive algorithm that uses a greedy approach to split the dataset. It begins with a single node and then recursively splits the data into two subsets based on the best split that maximizes the information gain. After the best splitting point is found, the algorithm moves onto the next node and splits it again. This process is repeated until all the nodes are split and the algorithm is complete.

The CART algorithm is a powerful algorithm for decision tree creation and provides an effective way to generate rules for predicting outcomes from data. It is a fast and reliable algorithm that can be used to solve both classification and regression problems.

7	**List down the different types of nodes in Decision Trees.**
ANSWER	**The different types of nodes in Decision Trees are:**

- **Decision Nodes:** These are the nodes that contain a testable condition or attribute. If the condition is satisfied, the corresponding branch is followed.
- **Chance Nodes:** These nodes contain randomness, and the branch followed is determined by the outcome of the random event.
- **End Nodes:** These are the nodes that mark the end of the tree, and they contain the prediction or the decision made by the algorithm.

8	**Which should be preferred among Gini impurity and Entropy?**
ANSWER	Gini impurity and Entropy are both measures of impurity in a data set, and each has its own advantages and disadvantages. Gini impurity is more computationally efficient, while Entropy requires more complex calculations. However, Entropy has the advantage of providing more information about the data set, so it's often the preferred measure. Ultimately, it comes down to the data set in question and the purpose of the analysis.

9	**Explain the difference between the CART and ID3 Algorithms**
ANSWER	The main difference between the two algorithms is that ID3 uses entropy to measure the impurity of the data points before splitting them into branches, while CART uses the Gini impurity measure. This means that ID3 is able to make more accurate decisions because it is able to measure the purity of the data more precisely. Additionally, CART is an iterative algorithm, while ID3 is not. This means that CART can keep building its decision tree until it is satisfied with the result, while ID3 will stop when it finds a good solution.
10	**Briefly explain the properties of Gini Impurity.**
ANSWER	Gini Impurity is a measure of the homogeneity of a dataset. It is used to assess the purity of a dataset by measuring the probability of misclassifying a randomly selected data sample. A Gini Impurity score of 0 represents a perfectly classified dataset—all samples have the same class. The higher the Gini Impurity, the more impure the dataset. Gini Impurity is calculated by subtracting the sum of the squared probability of each class within the dataset from 1. It provides a measure of the probability that a randomly selected data sample will be misclassified if it is randomly labelled according to the distribution of classes in the dataset.
11	**What do you understand about Information Gain? Also, explain the mathematical formulation associated with it.**
ANSWER	Information Gain is an important concept in machine learning and data science. It is used to improve the accuracy of predictions and help in decision-making by analyzing the

relationships between different features. In simple terms, it measures the amount of information that is gained by splitting the dataset according to the given feature.

The mathematical formulation associated with Information Gain is as follows:

Information Gain (IG) = Entropy(parent) − Weighted Sum of Entropy(children)

Where Entropy(parent) is the Entropy of the parent node, and Entropy(children) is the Entropy of the child nodes. The Weighted Sum of Entropy(children) is the sum of the Entropies of the children nodes multiplied by the probability of their occurrence in the dataset.

12 Do we require Feature Scaling for Decision Trees? Explain.

ANSWER   Feature scaling is not required for decision trees as the optimal split points of a decision tree will be determined by the training data, regardless of the range of values of the feature. Feature scaling is recommended for algorithms like linear regression and support vector machines, because these algorithms are sensitive to the scale of the feature values.

Feature scaling helps to reduce the impact of outliers and normalize the data. For example, if the range of values of one feature is much larger than the range of values of another feature, the larger feature will dominate in the calculations, leading to skewed results. Feature scaling helps to effectively identify the most important features for making decisions.

13 What are the disadvantages of Information Gain?

ANSWER Information gain is a popular method used to select and rank the best feature from a dataset based on the amount of information or entropy it provides. However, there are several drawbacks to this approach. One of the main disadvantages is that it tends to favor variables with a large number of unique values. Additionally, information gain can be computationally expensive, making it difficult to use in large datasets. Finally, information gain does not account for the correlation between two variables, which may result in incorrect feature selection.

14 List down the problem domains in which Decision Trees are most suitable.

ANSWER Decision trees are a type of supervised machine learning algorithms used in predictive analytics and are suitable for a wide range of problem domains.

They are generally used in classification problems such as customer segmentation, credit scoring, diagnosis of diseases, and fraud detection. Decision trees are also suitable for regression problems such as predicting customer lifetime value, customer churn, and stock market trend forecasting. In addition, decision trees are also suitable for optimization problems such as optimal portfolio selection and resource allocation. They are also used in natural language processing and computer vision tasks. Finally, decision trees can be used for feature selection, interpretation of models, and data exploration.

15 Explain the time and space complexity of training and testing with a Decision Tree.

ANSWER Training and testing a Decision Tree is a time- and space-efficient process. Training a Decision Tree involves building the tree structure in $O(n^2)$ time, where n is the number of training instances. This complexity is a result of the process of iteratively splitting the dataset into new partitions. Testing a Decision Tree is an $O(\log n)$ process, which is much more efficient compared to the training process. The space complexity of training and testing a Decision Tree is $O(n)$, as the tree structure required to store the model is linear in the number of training instances.

16 If it takes one hour to train a Decision Tree on a training set containing 1 million instances, roughly how much time will it take to train another Decision Tree on a training set containing 10 million instances?

ANSWER Training a Decision Tree on a large dataset can take a significant amount of time. Assuming the same complexity of the data, training a Decision Tree on a dataset containing 10 million instances will roughly take 10 times as long as training one on a dataset containing 1 million instances, or 10 hours.

17 How does a Decision Tree handle missing attribute values?

ANSWER When a Decision Tree encounters a missing attribute value, it is unable to accurately classify the data and must rely on alternate methods for dealing with the lack of data. There are several approaches for dealing with missing attribute values, including:

- **Ignoring the instance:** The instance can be ignored or removed from the dataset, as it cannot be used for classification.
- **Replacing the missing value with the most frequent value for that attribute:** The missing value can be replaced by the most frequent value for that attribute.
- **Using a bootstrapping technique:** This technique involves randomly selecting values from the training dataset to replace missing attribute values.
- **Using a predictive model such as regression or k-nearest neighbors:** A predictive model can be used to fill in missing attribute values.

Overall, by using one of the above approaches, a Decision Tree can successfully handle missing attribute values.

18. How does a Decision Tree handle continuous(numerical) features?

ANSWER A decision tree can handle continuous numerical features by binning them into discrete intervals, similar to how a histogram works. This process is known as discretization, and it works by dividing a range of values into a set of intervals. Each interval is then treated as a distinct category, and the decision tree will compare the input value to each category in order to determine which branch to follow. This allows the decision tree to process continuous numerical features, and make decisions based on the value of the feature.

19. What is the Inductive Bias of Decision Trees?

ANSWER The main idea behind decision trees is to use a series of questions (or tests) to determine the best decision or prediction. The inductive bias of decision trees dictates that the decision tree will be constructed in a way that favors the most general hypothesis that accurately predicts outcomes. This means that the decision tree will be constructed in a way that minimizes the number of mistakes it makes while still accurately predicting outcomes. This bias helps to prevent overfitting of the decision tree, which is an important factor in tree-based machine learning models.

20 Explain Feature Selection using the Information Gain/Entropy Technique.

ANSWER Feature selection is a process in machine learning used to determine which variables or attributes are most relevant to the outcome of an experiment. One of the most popular techniques used in feature selection is the information gain/entropy technique.

This technique works by determining how much information can be gained by using a given attribute to split the data. It is based on the idea that attributes that have the highest information gain should be used in the model and ignored if the information gain is low.

To calculate the information gain, the entropy of the system is first calculated. Entropy is a measure of the amount of disorder in a system. The entropy of a system is calculated by summing the negative of each probability multiplied by the log of that probability. After the entropy has been calculated, the information gain is calculated by subtracting the entropy of the system from the entropy of the system after the attribute has been used to split the data. The greater the difference between the two entropies, the higher the information gain.

The attribute with the highest information gain is then chosen as the best attribute to use in the model. This process is repeated until the desired number of attributes have been selected. Feature selection using the information gain/entropy technique is a popular, effective way to determine which variables are most important to the outcome of an experiment. By choosing the attributes with the highest information gain, the model can get the most accurate results and provide the best predictions.

21	**Compare the different attribute selection measures.**
ANSWER	There are many different attribute selection measures used for supervised machine learning algorithms, each of which has its own advantages and disadvantages. The three main measures are Information Gain (IG), Gain Ratio (GR), and Gini Index (GI).

Information Gain is based on the idea that the more information a feature can provide about the class labels, the more important that feature is. Thus, IG calculates the amount of information (entropy) a feature can offer. It is a popular choice because it is easy to compute and generally provides good results.

Gain Ratio is similar to Information Gain, but it also considers the split of the data due to the feature. This ensures that the feature is not only providing a lot of information, but also that it is evenly splitting the data. This means that GR can be more accurate than IG in certain cases.

Finally, Gini Index is based on the concept of purity. It calculates the probability of a certain class being predicted, given the value of a certain feature. Gini Index does not consider the number of classes, which can be beneficial in certain use cases.

In conclusion, all three measures have their advantages and disadvantages, depending on the use case. The best choice for a given application will depend on the specifics of the situation.

22 Does the Gini Impurity of a node lower or greater than that of its parent? Comment whether it is generally lower/greater, or always lower/greater?

ANSWER Gini Impurity is a measure of how homogeneous a node is in comparison to its parent. Generally speaking, the Gini Impurity of a node is lower than that of its parent. It is usually lower, as its parent is a more heterogeneous set and the node usually has a more homogenous set of values. However, it is not always lower, as the node may contain the same values as its parent.

23 Why do we require Pruning in Decision Trees? Explain.

ANSWER Pruning is an essential technique for Decision Trees that prevents overfitting. It is a way of reducing the complexity of the model by removing certain nodes from the tree. This helps to make the tree simpler, reducing its variance and making it more suitable for predictions. Pruning is done by replacing the subtrees with a leaf node containing the average of the target values of the examples in the subtree. This reduces the tree complexity, resulting in better generalization. Pruning helps to reduce the complexity of the model, making it easier to interpret and debug. It also reduces the computational cost of the model and helps to improve accuracy

24 Are Decision Trees affected by the outliers? Explain.

ANSWER Yes, decision trees are affected by outliers. Outliers are extreme values that are far away from the rest of the data. When creating decision trees, outliers can significantly reduce the accuracy of the tree because it may be difficult for the tree to accurately represent the data when it is influenced by the outliers.

Outliers can influence the tree in a number of ways. The decision tree will tend to split data near the outlier, resulting in a skewed tree that is not a good representation of the entire dataset. Additionally, outliers can cause the tree to overfit the data, as the tree may be too specific in its decision making, which can lead to poor generalization.

To address these issues, it is important to identify which values are outliers and handle them appropriately. This can be done by manually removing outliers or using techniques such as Winsorization or outlier replacement. These techniques can help to reduce the effect of the outliers and ensure the accuracy of the decision tree.

25 List down the advantages of the Decision Trees.

ANSWER Decision trees offer several advantages, including:

- **Easy to understand:** Decision trees are easy to understand and interpret. They are ideal for visualizing and analyzing complex problems as they are easy to explain to people.
- **Fast to use:** Decision trees are fast to use and generate results in a short amount of time. They are also relatively easy to set up, as they do not require a lot of data pre-processing.

- **Logical:** Decision trees are logical and can easily be used to make decisions. The result of a decision tree is always the same, no matter who is using it.
- **Powerful:** Decision trees are powerful tools for predicting outcomes. They are used in various fields, ranging from finance to healthcare.
- **Flexible:** Decision trees are flexible and can be customized to fit specific needs. They are particularly useful for problems where there are many variables and complex relationships between them.

26 **List out the disadvantages of the Decision Trees.**

ANSWER Though decision trees are a powerful machine learning tool with many advantages, there are some potential drawbacks to note as well.

- Decision trees can be prone to overfitting. This occurs when the training data is used to create the tree, but the model is too complex, with too many branches and nodes, which causes it to "memorize" the training data and not generalize to unseen data.
- Decision trees are also prone to instability, meaning that a slight change in the data can cause a large change in the tree structure, leading to different decisions.
- Decision trees can be computationally expensive. The time taken to construct the tree and make predictions can be long, especially if there are many features or data points.
- They can also be difficult to interpret, since the results are represented as a complex tree structure, rather than in a more straightforward numerical format.

27 Compare Linear Regression and Decision Trees
ANSWER

Linear Regression	Decision Trees
Linear regression attempts to find a linear relationship between the dependent variable and one or more independent variables.	Decision trees are a set of rules that can make decisions.
Linear regression is a simple yet powerful method for predicting a continuous dependent variable from one or more independent variables. It is the most widely used technique for regression tasks, as it is relatively easy to understand and interpret. Linear regression can be used for problems such as predicting housing prices or stock prices.	Decision trees are decision rules that are generated in a hierarchical structure. They are commonly used in classification tasks as they are good at finding patterns in data, and they can also be used for regression tasks. Decision trees do not require data to be linearly separable and can handle complex relationships between variables. They are also good at identifying outliers and can make predictions with small datasets.
Linear regression is a simple and powerful method for regression tasks.	Decision trees are better at finding patterns and are good for classification tasks.

CHAPTER 10

NEURAL NETWORKS

1 **What is Neural Network or Artificial Neural Network?**

ANSWER A neural network, also known as Artificial Neural Network is a machine learning program, or model, that makes decisions in a manner similar to the human brain, by using processes that mimic the way biological neurons work together to identify phenomena, weigh options and arrive at conclusions. At its core, a neural network is made up of interconnected units called neurons. Each neuron receives input, processes them, and produces an output.

Neurons are organized into layers. The three main types of layers are input layer, hidden layer and the output layer as shown in figure 10.1

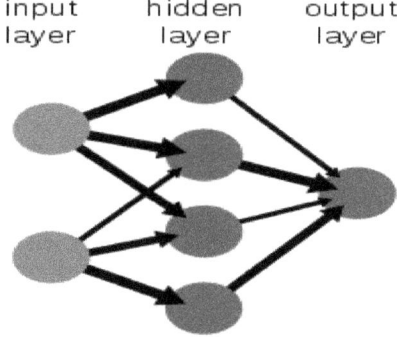

Figure 10.1: Representation of Neural Network

Input Layer: Receives the initial data.

Hidden Layers: Intermediate layers between the input and output layers. They perform computations on the input data.

Output Layer: Produces the final output or prediction.

2	**List the uses of Neural Network**
ANSWER	Artificial Neural Networks have several use cases across numerous domains: • Medical diagnosis by using medical image classification • Marketing by social network filtering • Stock market predication • Process and quality control • Chemical compound identification

3 **Discuss perceptron. Explain the different types of perceptrons.**

ANSWER Perceptron (also known as the McCulloch-Pitts neuron) is a supervised learning approach for binary classifiers. Using a vector of integers as input, a binary classifier is a function that can determine whether or not the input belongs to a particular class. It is a particular kind of linear classifier, or an algorithm for classifying data that bases its predictions on a linear predictor function that combines a set of weights with the feature vector.

The three main components of the perceptron are as shown in figure 10.2

Input Nodes or Input Layer: This layer accepts the initial data into the system for further processing. X1, X2, and X3 are the inputs given to the input layer.

Weights and Bias: Different weights is used to represent the importance of each input, and the sum of the values should be greater than the threshold value. W1, W2, and W3 are the weights.

The bias term is an additional parameter that's added to the sum of the weighted inputs before passing through the activation function. Mathematically, it's like having an extra input to the neuron that is always set to 1, which is then multiplied by the bias weight.

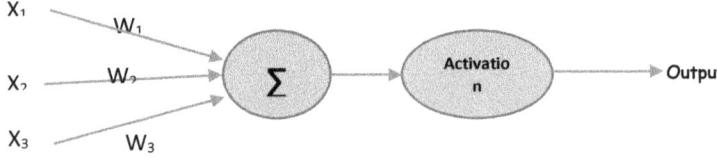

Figure 10.2: Representation of a neuron

Activation Function: This is the final component that helps to determine whether or not to fire the neuron. Activation function is also considered as a step function.

For example, consider the given values x1 = 1, x2 = 0, x3 = 1, w1 = 0.7, w2 = 0.6, w3 = 0.5 and the threshold value set is 1.5.

- X1 * w1 = 1 * 0.7 = 0.7
- X2 * w2 = 0 * 0.6 = 0
- X3 * w3 = 1 * 0.5 = 0.5

Summation of the results 0.7 + 0 + 0.5 = 1.2. So, activate the output if the sum is > 1.5 otherwise do not activate.

4 In a Neural Network, What Exactly Is the Function of the Activation Functions?

ANSWER An activation function is used at the most fundamental level to determine whether or not a neuron should activate. Any activation function can take the weighted sum of the inputs and the bias as an input. Activation functions include the step function, Sigmoid, ReLU, Tanh, and Softmax.

5 List out the types of activation functions

ANSWER The types of activation functions are:

- **Binary Step Function:** If the input is greater than or equal to the threshold value then the perceptron is activated else it is deactivated. Mathematically, $f(x) = 1, x>=0, f(x) = 0, x<0$. The binary function will not be useful if there are multiple classes in the target variable. The gradient of the function is 0 during the backpropagation process and the weights and biases do not get updated.

- **Linear Function:** Linear function can be used. For example, f(x) = ax, where a is the constant value. The linear function is ideal for simple tasks but cannot be used for complex patterns of data.
- **Sigmoid function:** the function is widely used for nor linear activation function. Mathematically, $f(x) = 1/(1+e^{-x})$ is used for the sigmoid function. The sigmoid function is not symmetric around 0.
- **Tanh function:** The tanh function is symmetric around the origin. Mathematically, f(x) = 2 * sigmoid(2x) -1. The tanh function is continuous and differentiable at all points. The gradient of the tanh function is steeper compared to the sigmoid function.
- **ReLU function:** ReLU stands for Rectified Linear Unit and it is a non-linear activation function. The function is activated only if the output of the linear transformation is greater than 0. Mathematically, f(x) = max(0,x). For some input values, the activation function never gets active. This is taken care by Leaky ReLU function. ReLU function should be used in the hidden layers only.
- **Leaky ReLU function:** Leaky ReLU function is an updated version of ReLU function. Mathematically represented as, f(x) = 0.01x, x<0 and f(x) = x, x>= 0
- **Parameterized ReLU function:** this function introduces a new parameter as a slope of the negative part of the function. Mathematically, f(x) = x, x>=0, f(x) = ax, x<0.
- **Exponential Linear Unit function:** ELU uses a log curve for defining the negative values. Mathematically, f(x) = x, x>=0, $f(x) = a(e^{x-1})$, x<0.

- **Swish function:** The values for swish activation function ranges from negative infinity to positive infinity. Mathematically, $f(x) = x*sigmoid(x)$ and $f(x) = x / (1-e^{-x})$. The swish function is not monotonic.
- **Softmax function:** This function is used for multiclass classification problems. This function returns the probability of the data point belonging to each class as shown in figure 10.3.

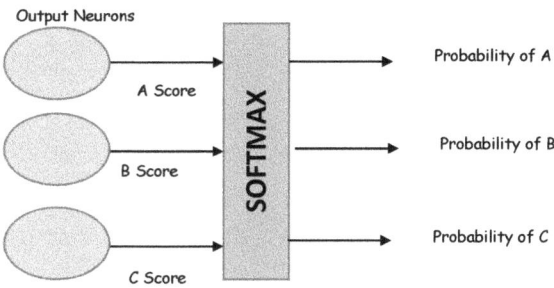

Figure 10.3: Representation of the Softmax function

6 Differentiate between neuron and perceptron.

ANSWER

Perceptron	Neuron
It is a machine learning algorithm that uses supervised learning of binary classifiers.	A neuron is a mathematical function modelled on the working of biological neurons
In Perceptron, the weight coefficient is automatically learned.	It is an elementary unit in an artificial neural network
Initially, weights are multiplied with input features, and then the decision is made whether or not the neuron is fired.	One or more inputs are separately weighted

The activation function applies a step rule to check whether the function is more significant than zero.	Inputs are summed and passed through a nonlinear function to produce output
The linear decision boundary is drawn, enabling the distinction between the two linearly separable classes +1 and -1.	Every neuron holds an internal state called activation signal
If the added sum of all input values is more than the threshold value, it must have an output signal; otherwise, no output will be shown.	Each connection link carries information about the input signal

7 Discuss cost function

ANSWER A cost function is required when the value predicted by the algorithm we develop is inaccurate. Cost function, often known as "loss" or "error," is a metric used to assess your model's efficiency and minimize the error factor. By comparing the actual value to the anticipated value, it determines the neural network's efficiency. Error = Predicted – Actual. During backpropagation, it is utilized to calculate the output layer's error. During the various training procedures, we feed this mistake back into the neural network.

8. Discuss Feed-Forward Networks

ANSWER A feedforward neural network (FNN) is a kind of artificial neural network in which there are no cycles in the connections between the nodes. This is called a feed-forward network because the data is flowing forward, with earlier neurons feeding, or delivering values to, later neurons as depicted in figure 10.4. There are no cycles or loops in the network.

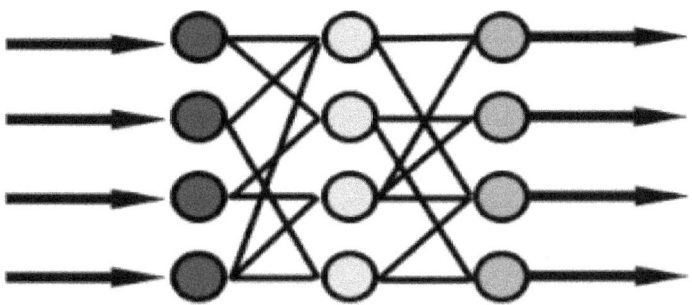

Figure 10.4: Schematic representation of feed forward networks

9. Explain Single layer and multi-layer perceptron model

ANSWER **Single Layer Perceptron Model**

A feed-forward network based on a threshold transfer function is known as a single layer perceptron (SLP). SLPs are the most basic type of artificial neural networks as shown in figure 10.5, and they can only classify cases that are linearly separable with a binary target (1, 0). The starting weights are chosen randomly since the single layer perceptron lacks a priori knowledge. SLP adds up all the weighted inputs, and if the sum exceeds a predefined threshold (output = 1), SLP is said to be triggered.

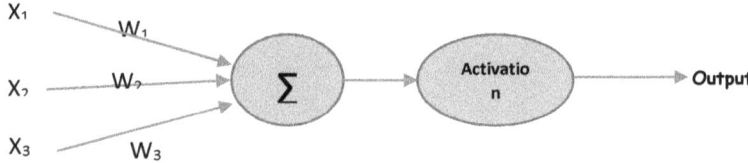

Figure 10.5 : Schematic representation of Single Layer perceptron model

Multi-Layer Perceptron Model

MLP is another name for multi-layer perceptron. Any input dimension is transformed to the desired dimension via fully connected dense layers. Having many layers in a neural network is known as multi-layer perceptron. The outputs of some neurons become the inputs of other neurons when we join neurons to form a neural network.

There are three inputs and hence three input nodes in the multi-layer perceptron, and three nodes in the hidden layer. There are two output nodes since the output layer produces two outputs. In the diagram 10.6, the nodes in the input layer forward their output to each of the three nodes in the hidden layer, and in a similar manner, the hidden layer processes the data before sending it to the output layer. Between the input and output layers, there can be one or more layers of neurons. The nodes in the input layer receive input and forward it for further processing. The sigmoid activation function is used by each node in the multi-layer perception.

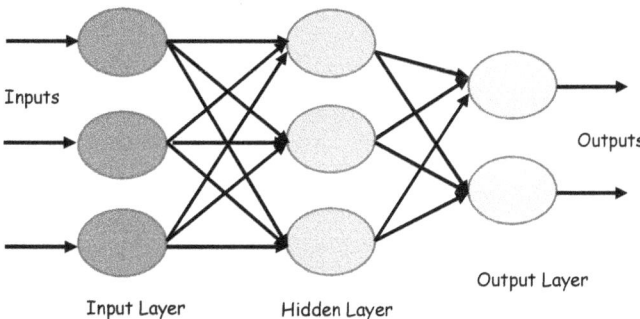

Figure 10.6: Schematic representation of multi-layer perceptron model

10 **List out some algorithms used for Initializing the weights.**

ANSWER Some algorithms that selects the initial values from the uniform distribution are:
- Gradient descent algorithm
- The LeCun Uniform algorithm
- Glorot Uniform algorithm
- He Uniform algorithm

11 **What is the purpose of using back propagation algorithm?**

ANSWER The weights and biases in an artificial neural network are initialised at random. The neural network most likely produces incorrect results because of random initialization. Error levels need to be as low as feasible. In order to lower these error values, we therefore need a system that can compare the neural network's desired output with the network's error-filled output and alter the weights and biases of the network as necessary to bring the desired output closer after each iteration. We train the network in order for it to update the weights and biases using back propagation in order to do this. This is how the backpropagation algorithm operates.

12 Explain backpropagation algorithm in detail

ANSWER Backpropagation is a fundamental algorithm used in training artificial neural networks. It's essentially a way to adjust the weights of the connections between neurons in a neural network based on the error of the network's output compared to the expected output. Here's a detailed explanation of how backpropagation works:

Step 1: Forward Pass

- The input data is fed into the neural network.
- The data passes through each layer of the network, and calculations are performed to produce an output.
- The output is compared to the expected output (ground truth) to compute the error using a predefined loss function, such as mean squared error (MSE) for regression tasks or categorical cross-entropy for classification tasks.

Step 2: Backward Pass

- Backpropagation starts with the output layer and moves backward through the network.
- The error is propagated backward from the output layer to the hidden layers, layer by layer.
- At each layer, the algorithm computes the gradient of the error with respect to the weights of the connections between neurons using the chain rule of calculus.
- The gradients indicate how much the error would decrease if the weights were adjusted slightly.
- These gradients are used to update the weights in a way that minimizes the error, typically using an optimization algorithm such as gradient descent.

Step 3: Weight Update

- Once the gradients of the error with respect to the weights are computed for all connections in the network, the weights are updated.
- The weights are adjusted in the direction that reduces the error, typically by subtracting a fraction of the gradient multiplied by a learning rate hyperparameter.
- The learning rate controls the size of the update steps and is crucial for ensuring convergence and stability during training.

Step 4: Iteration

- The forward pass followed by the backward pass and weight updates constitute one iteration (or one training step) of the backpropagation algorithm.
- This process is repeated iteratively for multiple epochs (passes through the entire dataset) until the network's performance converges or reaches a satisfactory level.

Step 5: Mini-Batch Training

- In practice, backpropagation is often performed on mini-batches of data rather than the entire dataset at once.
- This approach reduces the computational cost and helps in generalizing better to unseen data.

Step 6: Regularization

- Backpropagation can be augmented with regularization techniques such as L1 or L2 regularization to prevent overfitting and improve the generalization performance of the neural network.

13 Define Hyperparameters. What are the hyperparameters of Artificial Neural Networks?

ANSWER When tuning a neural network, hyperparameters are the parameters that are adjusted. The parameters are:

- **Learning Rate:** is a tuning parameter in an optimization algorithm that determines the step size at each iteration while moving toward a minimum of a loss function and is symbolised by the lower-case Greek letter η (eta).
- **Momentum:** It is an extension to the gradient descent optimization process can overcome the oscillations of noisy gradients and ride across areas of the search space that are flat. This allows the search to develop inertia in a particular direction in the search space.
- **Epoch:** Total number of iterations of all the training data in one cycle for training the machine learning model.

14 Define optimizers.

ANSWER The tools used to automate some of the work of finding the best learning rate automatically over time. Collectively, these algorithms are called optimizers.

15 Explain regularization.

ANSWER Regularization procedures are strategies that prevent overfitting from occurring right away. They give us the ability to train for longer periods of time before overfitting has a significant negative influence, giving the network additional training time to enhance their performance.

The two regularization methods used are dropout and Batchnorm.

Dropout: Dropout is a regularization technique that is typically used as a dropout layer in deep networks ensuring that no units are co-dependent with one another. Because it cannot perform any computations on its own, it is also known as an accessory layer or supplemental layer.

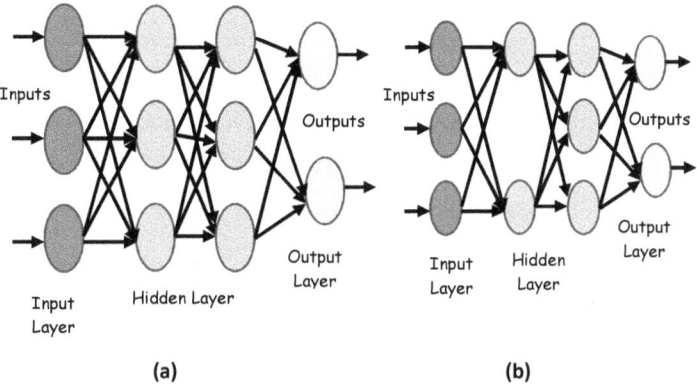

Figure 10.7(a & b): Representation of Regularization Methods

In the above image, dropout on (a) network is applied and in the second hidden layer of a neuron network.

Batchnorm: Batchnorm is a neural network layer that modifies the values that come out of a layer. It performs some computation, though there are no parameters for us to specify. It makes artificial neural network faster and more stable through normalization of the layers' inputs by re-centering and re-scaling.

CHAPTER 11

DEEP LEARNING

1 **What are the distinguishing characteristics and applications of Artificial Intelligence (AI), Machine Learning (ML), and Deep Learning (DL)?**

ANSWER Unlike the intelligence demonstrated by humans and animals, Artificial Intelligence (AI) as shown in figure 11.1 pertains to computers' ability to perceive, synthesize, and infer information. Examples of tasks in which AI excels include speech recognition, computer vision, language translation, and various forms of input processing.

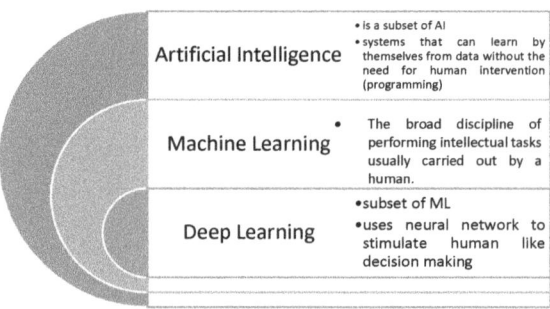

Figure 11.1: AI vs ML vs DL

A subset within artificial intelligence (AI), Machine Learning (ML) is an area of research concentrated on comprehending and creating "learning" techniques. These methods utilize data to improve performance across specific sets of experiences and tasks.

Deep Learning (DL - also known as deep structured learning) is a subset of machine learning that is based on artificial neural networks and representation learning.

2 **Define Deep Learning.**

ANSWER Deep learning, commonly referred to as "deep structured learning," is one of several machine learning techniques built on representation learning and layered artificial neural networks. Building an interconnected network of computing units is the foundation of deep learning algorithms as represented in figure 11.2. Artificial neurons, which are tiny computation bundles, are the basic building block of these networks. The neurons are typically organized into multiple layers, especially in deep learning

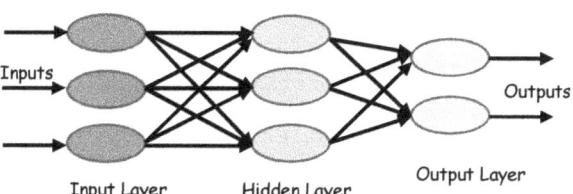

Figure 11.2: Schematic view of deep neural network

3	**List out the types of algorithms used in Deep Learning.**
ANSWER	Types of algorithms used in Deep Learning are
- Convolutional Neural Network (CNN)
- Long Short-Term Memory Network (LSTM)
- Recurrent Neural Network
- Generative Adversarial Network (GAN)
- Radial Basis Function Network (RBFN)
- Multilayer Perceptron (MPL)
- Self Organizing Map (SOM)
- Deep Belief Networks (DBN)
- Restricted Boltzmann Machines (RBM)
- Autoencoders
4	**Discuss Convolutional Neural Network (CNN)**
ANSWER	A convolutional neural network (CNN, or ConvNet) is a class of artificial neural network (ANN) and a deep learning algorithm, most commonly applied to analyze visual imagery. The CNN takes an input image, assigns importance (learnable weights and biases) to the various aspects of the image, and can differentiate one from the other. The neurons in a convolution neural network are arranged in three dimensions rather than the typical two-dimensional array. VGG16 (Visual Geometry Group) network is one of the most popularly used CNN for classifying networks.

5 Explain the working of CNN

ANSWER CNN consists of a sequence of layers, and every layer transforms one volume of data to another through a differentiated function. The types of layers used in CNN are as follows. For example, consider an example where the CNN is running on an image of dimension 32*32*3, where 32 and 32 are the length and height of the image and 3 is the depth (that is., images have red, blue, and green channels)

Input Layer: This layer holds the raw input of the image with 32 * 32 * 3

Convolutional Layer: The dot product between all filters and image patches is computed in this layer to determine the output volume. If we apply a total of 12 filters, then we, will have the dimensions 32 x 32 x 12 as output for this layer.

Activation function layer: The output of the convolution layer will be subjected to an element-wise activation function in this layer. The following activation functions are frequently used: Tanh, Leaky RELU, RELU: max (0, x), Sigmoid: 1/(1+e-x), etc. Since the volume is constant, the output volume will have the following dimensions: 32 x 32 x 12.

Pool Layer: This layer is added to the CNN regularly, and its primary goal is to lower the size of the volume, which speeds up computation, saves memory, and avoids overfitting. Pooling layers are classified into two types: max pooling and average pooling. If we use a maximum pool with 2 x 2 filters and stride 2, the volume will be 16x16x12.

Fully Connected Layer: This layer, which is a typical neural network layer, uses the data from the layer above to compute the class scores and output a 1-D array with a size equal to the number of classes.

6   **Explain the two different types of pooling used in CNN**

ANSWER   The two types of pooling used in CNN are max pooling and average pooling. Max pooling returns the maximum value from the portion of the image covered by the kernel and the average pooling returns the average of all the values from the portion of the image covered by the kernel as shown in figure 11.3.

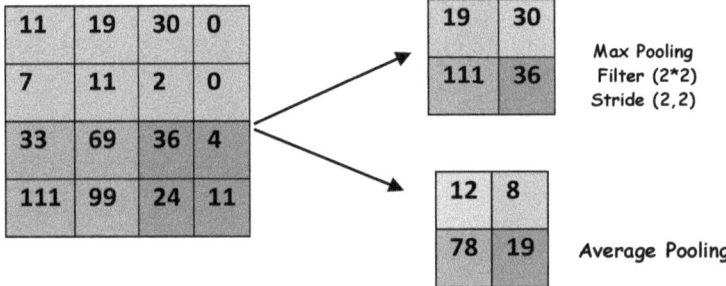

7   **Describe the filters that are used in CNN**

ANSWER   Filters (Multi-dimensional data) are used in the Convolution layer, which helps in extracting features from the input image. During training, a CNN obtains a set of weights for each filter. The filter's ability to identify patterns in the incoming data is controlled by these weights. For instance, if the filter's weights are calibrated to identify horizontal lines, it will actively search for such lines in the input picture; if the weights are calibrated to identify diagonal lines, it will do the same for those lines.

Some of the filters used here are:
- Gaussian Blur filter
- Prewitt filter
- Sobel filter
- Laplacian filter
- Krisch Compass filters

8 Explain the working of the Laplacian filter in CNN

ANSWER Consider the Laplacian filter figure 11.4 (a) which is applied to the image figure 11.4 (b). The Laplacian filter is a single filter that detects edges of different orientations. It computes the second-order derivatives of the pixel value. Each element of the input data is multiplied by the filter's coefficients as the filter matrix is slid over the data.

Step 1:

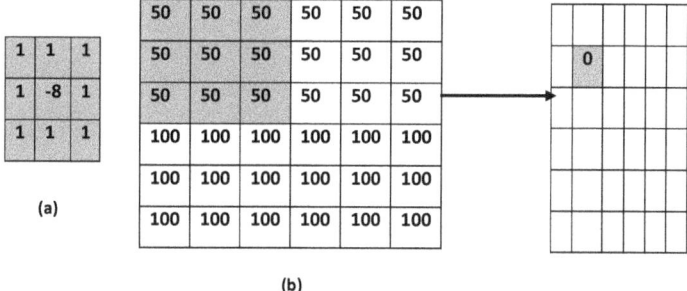

Figure 11.4 (a & b): Laplacian filter and the image representation

$$50*1 + 50*1 + 50*1 + 50*1 + (-8)*50 + 50*1 + 50*1 + 50*1 + 50*1 = 0$$

Step 2:

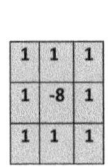

$$50*1 + 50*1 + 50*1 + 50*1 + (-8)*50 + 50*1 + 50*1 + 50*1 + 50*1 = 0$$

Step 3:

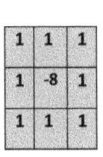

$$50*1 + 50*1 + 50*1 + 50*1 + (-8)*50 + 50*1 + 50*1 + 50*1 + 50*1 = 0$$

Step 4:

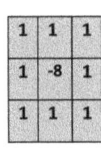
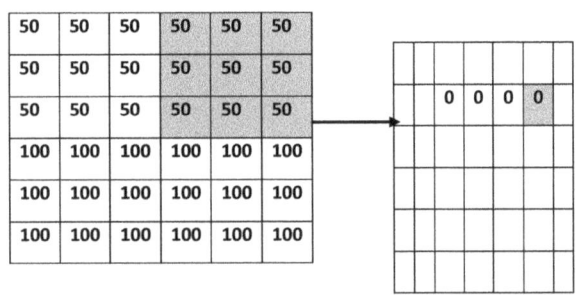

$$50*1 + 50*1 + 50*1 + 50*1 + (-8)*50 + 50*1 + 50*1 + 50*1 + 50*1 = 0$$

Step 5:

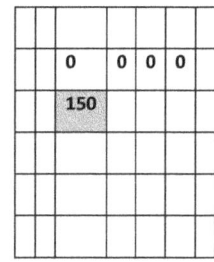

$$50*1 + 50*1 + 50*1 + 50*1 + (-8)*50 + 50*1 + 100*1 + 100*1 + 100*1 = 150$$

Sliding the filter and continuing it further we get the final matrix as shown below. To get all the cell values, we can take the padding values as 0, constant values, or the same values can be repeated.

0	0	0	0
150	150	150	150
-150	-150	-150	-150
0	0	0	0

9. What do you understand by Fully Connected Layers (FC)?

ANSWER Fully connected neural network consists of a series of fully connected layers as shown in figure 11.5. Fully connected layers flatten the output and turns them into a single vector. If there are three neurons in the FC layer, four neurons in the preceding layer, then each neuron in the FC layer has four inputs, one from each neuron in the preceding layer, for a total of 3 * 4 = 12 connections, each with an associated weight. If the layer is made up of only fully connected layer, then it is called fully connected network.

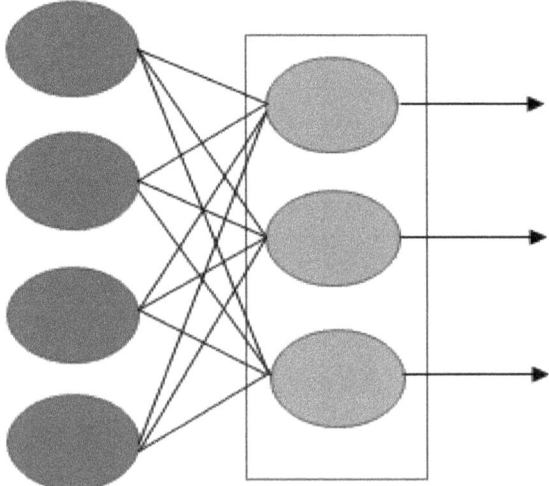

Figure 11.5: Representation of Fully Connected Layer

A fully connected layer multiplies the input by a weight matrix and then adds a bias vector. In a fully connected layer, each neuron applies a linear transformation to the input vector through a weight's matrix. As a result, all possible connections layer-to-layer are present, meaning every input of the input vector influences every output of the output vector.

10	**Identify the uses of Fourier transform in deep learning**
ANSWER	

- Edge identification, image filtering, picture reconstruction, and image compression are just a few examples of how the Fourier transform is frequently employed in image analysis. A case in point is the images from transmission electron microscopy that have undergone a Fourier transformation can be used to examine the periodicity of the materials. Periodicity means pattern. Data's Fourier transformation can increase the amount of information that can be accessed about the sample being studied.
- A Fourier transform involves converting any straightforward or intricate pattern into the basic sinusoidal waves from which it is constructed.
- Convolutions account for 90% of CNNS computations, and while numerous methods have been developed to lessen the computational burden of such operations, one of them is the Fast Fourier Transform (FFT)
- The input and filter matrices are transformed into the frequency domain by FFT, allowing multiplications to be performed instead of convolutions. The output is then transformed using Inverse FFT back into the time domain (IFFT).
- Fourier transform required much more memory space and bandwidth

11 List out the advantages and disadvantages of Deep Learning

ANSWER

Advantages of Deep Learning

- Parameters are automatically extracted from the given data and they are optimally tuned to get the desired outcome.
- The same neural network can be used to different applications and data types.
- The deep learning architecture is flexible to be adapted to new problems in the future.
- Problems are solved on an end to end basis.

Disadvantages of Deep Learning

- It requires a very large amount of data to perform better
- It is expensive to train complex data models
- Knowledge about the topology, training method and the parameters are required to select the correct deep learning tool.
- Deep learning techniques sometimes cannot provide conclusions in cross-disciplinary problems.

12 Explain Lossless Vs Lossy Encoding

ANSWER

Lossy Encoding	Lossless Encoding
Permanently removes the data from the file	Restores and rebuilds compressed data
It is used when file information loss is acceptable	Used when file information loss is not acceptable.
Quality degrades due to higher rate of compression	No loss in quality. Slight decreases in file sizes. Compressed files are larger than lossy files.

13 **Define autoencoder and the uses of autoencoder.**

ANSWER Autoencoder is a mechanism for compressing input data, so it takes up less disk space and can be communicated more quickly. The autoencoder get its name from the idea that it automatically learns, by virtue of training, how best to encode, or represent the input data.

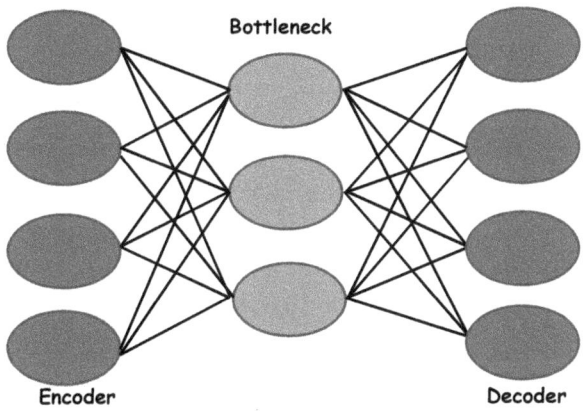

Figure 11.6: Architecture of encoder

Autoencoders is used for two types of work: reducing the dimensionality of the dataset, and removing the noise from the dataset. Autoencoder is a type of artificial neural network used to learn data encodings. The architecture of encoder is as shown in figure 11.6 and consists of three layers: the encoder, the bottleneck and the decoder.

Encoder: It is a module that includes a set of convolutional blocks and pooling modules that encodes a representation of the training and testing input data that is often several orders of magnitude smaller than the input data. The output from the encoder is sent to the bottleneck

Bottleneck: The most crucial component of the network is the module that houses the compressed knowledge representations.

Decoder: Decoder is a component that helps the network "unpack" the representations of knowledge and put the data back together from its encoded form. A ground truth is then used to compare the output.

14 Why cannot autoencoders do lossless compression in machine learning?

ANSWER A neural network is not designed for accurate representations; instead, it learns to approximatively represent functions, in this example, the identity function. So, it is impossible to expect to receive the original input by design.

15 List out some autoencoders

ANSWER Some of the encoders used are
- Undercomplete autoencoders
- Sparse autoencoders
- Conventional autoencoders
- Contractive autoencoders
- Denoising autoencoders
- Variational autoencoders

16 Describe Convolutional Autoencoders

ANSWER A neural network called a convolutional autoencoder is trained to replicate the input image in the output layer (it is a specific instance of an unsupervised learning model). A ConvNet encoder that creates a low-dimensional representation of an image is used to process an image. Using this compressed image as a starting point, the decoder—another example ConvNet—recreates the original image. Figure 11.7 displays the architecture of convolutional autoencoder.

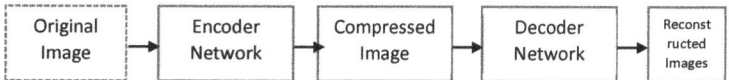

Figure 11.7: architecture of convolutional autoencoder

Consider an example of convolution to scale 28 by 28 image in stages until it's just 7 by 7. The convolutions will use 3 by 3 filters, and zero-padding. The convolutional encoder will start with 16 filters and follow it with a maximum pooling layer with a 2 by 2 cell, giving the tensor by 14 * 14 * 16. Another convolution is applied, this time with 8 filters, and follow that with pooling, producing a tensor that's 7 * 7 * 8. The final encoder layer uses three filters, producing a tensor that is 7 * 7 * 3 at the bottleneck. Hence, the bottleneck represents the 768 inputs with 7 * 7 * 3 = 147 latent variables. The flattening of the image is carried out before the bottleneck.

The decoder network runs the process in reverse. The first upsampling layer produces the layer that is 14 * 14 * 3. The following convolutional and upsampling gives a tensor that is 28 * 28 * 16, and the final convolution produces a tensor of shape 28 * 28 * 1. Lastly, the reshaping of the image is done.

17   What is Variational Autoencoders?

ANSWER   A variational autoencoders (VAE) shares the same general architecture as that of Convolutional Autoencoders but does an even better job of clumping the latent variables and filling up the latent space. VAE's also have some unpredictability. VAE uses probabilistic ideas in the encoding stage.

18   What is RNN?

ANSWER   Recurrent neural network (RNN) is a type of neural network that contains loops, allowing information to be stored within the network as shown in figure 11.8. In short, RNN use their reasoning from previous experiences to inform the upcoming events. RNN is used in language translation, natural language processing (nlp), speech recognition, and image captioning.

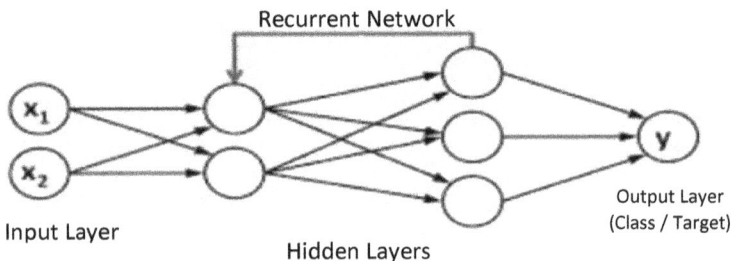

Figure 11.8: Architecture of Recurrent Neural Network

19   List out the disadvantages of RNN

ANSWER
- This neural network's calculation speed is slow.
- Training might be difficult.
- When applying the activation functions, processing large sequences becomes quite tiresome.
- It has difficulties like Exploding and Gradient Vanishing.

20 Differentiate between the Exploding Gradient and Gradient Vanishing phenomena in the context of neural networks.

ANSWER When huge error gradients build and result in very large modifications to neural network model weights during training, this is known as exploding gradients. Gradients are utilized to update network weights during training, although this process works best when the updates are minimal and controlled.

As the number of layers in the network increases, the value of the product of derivatives drops until the partial derivative of the loss function approaches a value close to zero, at which point the partial derivative vanishes. This is known as the vanishing gradient problem.

21 Explain the importance of LSTM

ANSWER Long Short-Term Memory (LSTM) are a form of recurrent neural network invented in the 1990s by Sepp Hochreiter and Juergen Schmidhuber, and now widely used for image, sound and time series analysis, because they help solve the vanishing gradient problem by using a memory gate.

The block diagram of LSTM is as shown in the figure 11.9. The LSTM uses three internal neural networks. The first is used to remove or forget information from the state that is no longer needed. The second inserts new information the cell wants to remember. The third network presents a version of the internal state as the cell's output.

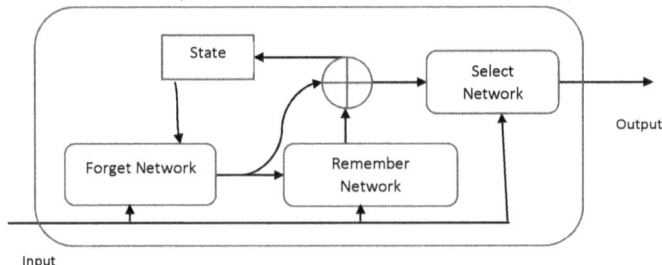

The convention is that forgetting a number simply means moving it towards zero, and remembering a new number means adding it into the appropriate location in the state memory.

22 Describe Boltzmann Machine

ANSWER A Boltzmann machine is a stochastic spin-glass model with an external field, which is a Sherrington-Kirkpatrick model. The machine's units produce binary results, and the global energy in a Boltzmann machine is identical in form to that of Hopfield networks and Ising models. It is a network of symmetrically connected, neuron-like units that make stochastic decisions about whether to be on or off. The learning algorithm is very slow in networks with many layers of feature detectors, but it is fast in "restricted Boltzmann machines" that have a single layer of feature detectors.

Boltzmann machines are used to solve two quite different computational problems: a search problem and a learning problem. For a search problem, the weights on the connections are fixed and are used to represent a cost function. For a learning problem, the Boltzmann machine is shown a set of binary data vectors and it must learn to generate these vectors with high probability. The Boltzmann machine is composed of a shallow two-layer neural network and is the building blocks of a deeper network.

23	**Describe the different types of CNN**
ANSWER	There are different types of CNNs, each with its own unique characteristics and uses. The most common types of CNNs are:

- **LeNet-5:** This is the original CNN developed by Yann LeCun in the 1990s. It is still widely used for image classification, such as identifying handwritten digits.
- **AlexNet:** This was developed by Alex Krizhevsky in 2012 and was the first widely used deep learning model. It is used for image classification and object detection.
- **VGGNet:** Developed by Karen Simonyan and Andrew Zisserman in 2014, this is a deep convolutional neural network with a large number of layers. It is often used for image classification.
- **GoogLeNet:** Developed by Google in 2014, this network is much deeper than most other CNNs and is often used for image classification and object detection.

24	**Differentiate between FNN and RNN**
ANSWER	FNN (Feed-forward Neural Network) and RNN (Recurrent Neural Network) are both neural networks which are used to process data using artificial intelligence.

FNNs have a feed-forward architecture, meaning that the data is inputted and processed through its layers of neurons without any feedback loops. This type of network is used for basic classification tasks, such as image and text recognition, where the output is based on the inputted data without changing over time.

On the other hand, RNNs have a recurrent architecture. This means that the output of one layer of neurons is fed back into the same layer, creating a feedback loop. This type of network is used for more complex tasks, such as language processing, where the output depends on previous inputs and changes over time. RNNs are also used for problems that are sequential in nature, like video and audio recognition, where the output is determined not only by the current input but by the sequence of inputs.

25 Define Hyperparameters

ANSWER Hyperparameters are variables that are used to fine-tune machine learning algorithms, such as the degree of regularization or the learning rate. They are usually determined empirically by running the algorithm with different values and seeing which produces the best results. Hyperparameters can make a huge difference in the performance of a model, so finding the optimal ones is essential for obtaining the best results.

26 List out the differences between bagging and boosting

ANSWER Bagging and boosting are two popular techniques for ensemble learning, a type of machine learning where multiple models are combined to improve accuracy.

Bagging	Boosting
Bagging uses the same type of model to make multiple predictions.	Boosting uses the same dataset with different algorithms to improve the accuracy of the model.

Bagging is an ensemble technique that involves training multiple models with different samples of data and then averaging the results.	Boosting is an ensemble technique that involves combining multiple weak learners (or weak models) to produce a strong model.
This type of model is useful when dealing with large datasets and complex models. By training multiple models with different samples, bagging reduces the chance of overfitting and makes the model more robust and accurate.	Boosting involves training multiple models with the same dataset. Each model is trained with a different algorithm, and each model is used to improve the accuracy of the model.
Bagging involves training multiple models with different samples of data and averaging the results.	Boosting involves training multiple models with the same dataset with different algorithms and using each model to improve the accuracy of the model.

27   **Explain transfer learning. Name a few commonly used transfer learning models**

ANSWER   Transfer learning is a machine learning technique where a model trained on one task is used as the starting point for a model on a second task. Transfer learning conserves training time, as the model is already partially trained.

Common transfer learning models include ResNet, Inception, and Xception. These models work well in computer vision tasks and are pretrained on ImageNet, a large-scale dataset of over 14 million images. Other popular models are BERT, GPT-2, and XLNet, which are useful for natural language processing tasks and are pretrained on a corpus of text data.

28 **What is the necessity of employing transfer learning?**

ANSWER Many deep neural networks trained on image data exhibit a common phenomenon: in their early layers, they endeavor to grasp low-level features such as edge detection, color recognition, and variations in intensity. These features seem to lack specificity to any particular dataset or task, as they are essential for various image processing tasks, whether detecting a horse or a unicorn. Consequently, these features emerge irrespective of the specific cost function or image dataset being used. Therefore, the learning of such features in one task, such as detecting unicorns, can be beneficially applied to other tasks, like identifying dog.

29 **Explain the working of Transfer Learning.**

ANSWER Transfer learning involves leveraging knowledge gained from training one model on a particular task and applying it to a different but related task or domain. Here's how it generally works:

1. **Pre-trained Model:** Initially, a deep learning model is trained on a large dataset for a specific task, such as image classification or natural language processing. This model is typically trained on a massive dataset, such as ImageNet for image tasks or Common Crawl for text tasks. The trained model is known as the pre-trained model.

2. **Feature Extraction:** In transfer learning, the pre-trained model's learned features are extracted from one or more of its layers. These features represent abstract and hierarchical representations of the input data. For example, in an image classification task, the earlier layers of a pre-trained convolutional neural network (CNN) might have learned to detect simple features like edges and textures, while deeper layers may have learned more complex features like shapes and objects.

3. **Transfer to New Task/Knowledge:** These extracted features are then used as the input to a new model, which is trained on a smaller dataset specific to the new task or domain. This new model is often referred to as the target model. By initializing the target model with the pre-trained weights and fine-tuning it on the new dataset, the model can learn to adapt its parameters to the new task more quickly and effectively.

4. **Fine-tuning:** Optionally, the transferred model can be fine-tuned by continuing the training process on the new dataset. During fine-tuning, the weights of the transferred model are adjusted to better fit the new task or domain. Fine-tuning allows the model to learn task-specific features while retaining the general knowledge gained from the pre-trained model.

30 Describe the different types of Transfer Learning.

ANSWER Transfer learning can be categorized into different types based on the relationship between the source and target domains, as well as the specific techniques used. Here are some common types of transfer learning:

1. **Inductive Transfer Learning:**
   a. **Domain Adaptation:** In this type of transfer learning, the source and target domains are related, but there may be differences in their distributions. The goal is to adapt the model learned on the source domain to perform well on the target domain by reducing the distribution discrepancy.
   b. **Cross-Domain Transfer:** Transfer learning between domains that are unrelated. This involves transferring knowledge from a source domain with abundant data to a target domain with limited labeled data.
2. **Transductive Transfer Learning:**
   - **Instance-Based Transfer:** Transfer learning where knowledge is transferred between tasks or domains based on specific instances or examples. This approach focuses on transferring knowledge at the instance level rather than generalizing across domains.
3. **Sequential Transfer Learning:**
   - **Pre-training and Fine-tuning:** In this approach, a model is first pre-trained on a large dataset or task and then fine-tuned on a specific target task or dataset. The pre-trained model serves as a starting point, and its parameters are adjusted during fine-tuning to better fit the target task.

4. **Multi-Task Learning:**
   - **Joint Training:** Transfer learning where a model is trained to perform multiple tasks simultaneously. By sharing representations across tasks, the model can leverage knowledge learned from one task to improve performance on other related tasks.
5. **Self-Transfer Learning:**
   - **Knowledge Distillation:** Transfer learning where knowledge is transferred from a large, complex model (teacher model) to a smaller, more efficient model (student model). This approach aims to distill the knowledge learned by the teacher model into the student model, improving its performance and efficiency.
6. **Unsupervised Transfer Learning:**
   - **Feature Representation Learning:** Transfer learning where knowledge is transferred by learning generic feature representations from unlabeled data in the source domain. These learned representations can then be used to improve performance on supervised tasks in the target domain.
7. **Semi-Supervised Transfer Learning:**
   - **Combination of Supervised and Unsupervised Learning:** Transfer learning where labeled data is available in both the source and target domains, but the amount of labeled data in the target domain is limited. This approach combines supervised learning on the labeled data with unsupervised learning or self-training on the unlabeled data to improve model performance.

31 Describe the difference between transductive transfer learning and inductive transfer learning.

ANSWER

Transductive Transfer Learning	Inductive Transfer Learning
Transductive transfer learning focuses on transferring knowledge between tasks or domains based on specific instances or examples.	Inductive transfer learning involves transferring knowledge from a source domain to a target domain where the domains are related but may have differences in their distributions.
Instance-Level Transfer: In transductive transfer learning, the transfer of knowledge occurs at the level of individual instances or examples. This means that the knowledge learned from the source domain is directly applied to specific instances in the target domain without explicitly learning a general mapping between the domains.	Domain-Level Transfer: Inductive transfer learning focuses on transferring knowledge at the level of entire domains. This means that the knowledge learned from the source domain is generalized and applied to the target domain, with the goal of adapting the model to perform well on the target domain.
Unlike inductive transfer learning, transductive transfer learning does not involve generalizing knowledge across entire domains. Instead, it operates on a case-by-case basis, transferring knowledge only to the instances present in the target domain.	Unlike transductive transfer learning, inductive transfer learning aims to generalize knowledge across entire domains, allowing the model to adapt to differences between the source and target domains and perform well on the target task.
Transductive transfer learning is particularly useful when the target domain has limited labeled data.	Inductive transfer learning is commonly used in scenarios where the source and target domains are related but have different distributions.

32   **Describe the process of fine tuning a pre-trained neural network.**

ANSWER   Fine-tuning a pre-trained neural network involves adapting a model that has been previously trained on a source task or dataset to a new target task or dataset. This process typically consists of several steps:

- **Selecting a Pre-trained Model:** Choose a pre-trained neural network model that was trained on a large dataset for a related task. Common choices include convolutional neural networks (CNNs) for image-related tasks and pre-trained transformer models like BERT for natural language processing tasks.
- **Modifying the Model Architecture:** Depending on the specific requirements of the target task, you may need to modify the architecture of the pre-trained model. This could involve adding or removing layers, adjusting the number of neurons in certain layers, or changing activation functions.
- **Freezing Layers:** Freeze the weights of the pre-trained layers in the model to prevent them from being updated during training. Since these layers have already learned meaningful representations from the source data, freezing them helps to preserve this knowledge and prevents overfitting on the target data.
- **Adding New Layers:** Add new layers on top of the pre-trained layers to adapt the model to the target task. These new layers are typically randomly initialized and trained from scratch. The number of new layers and their architectures can vary depending on the complexity of the target task.

- **Training on Target Data:** Train the modified model on the target dataset using labeled data. During training, the gradients are backpropagated through the network, and the weights of the new layers are updated to minimize a loss function that measures the difference between the model predictions and the ground truth labels.
- **Fine-tuning Parameters:** Optionally, fine-tune the parameters of the pre-trained layers by unfreezing them and allowing them to be updated during training. This step can help further adapt the model to the target task by allowing it to adjust its learned representations based on the target data.
  - **Regularization and Optimization:** Apply regularization techniques such as dropout or weight decay to prevent overfitting during training. Additionally, use optimization algorithms such as stochastic gradient descent (SGD) or Adam to update the model parameters efficiently.
  - **Monitoring Performance:** Monitor the performance of the fine-tuned model on a separate validation dataset to ensure that it is generalizing well to the target task. Adjust hyperparameters or training strategies as needed to improve performance.
  - **Evaluation:** Finally, evaluate the fine-tuned model on a held-out test dataset to assess its performance and generalization ability. Compare its performance with baseline models or other approaches to determine its effectiveness for the target task.

33. Discuss the advantages and disadvantages of transfer learning.

ANSWER

Advantages of Transfer Learning

- Improved Performance with Limited Data
- Faster Training and Convergence
- Generalization Across Domains
- Reduced Computational Costs
- Domain-Specific Knowledge Transfer

Disadvantages of Transfer Learning

- Domain Mismatch and Distribution Shift.
- Risk of Overfitting
- Transferability Constraints
- Bias Amplification
- Model Interpretability

34. Discuss capsule neural network

ANSWER A capsule neural network, or CapsNet, is a type of deep learning network that is based on a group of neurons referred to as capsules. Capsules are neurons that represent higher-level features, such as parts of an object or an entire object, and are connected to other capsules in a hierarchical manner.

CapsNets work by first recognizing the objects present in an image or video, then routing information among the capsules based on the relationships between the objects. Each capsule receives input from the previous layer and generates an output vector that contains information about the object's pose, size, and other properties. This output vector is then sent to the next layer of capsules, where it is used to identify more complex objects.

35 List out the advantages of capsule neural network

ANSWER The advantage of using a CapsNet over traditional deep learning networks is that the networks are able to build representations of objects that are more robust to changes in scale, orientation, and viewpoint. This means that CapsNets can better identify objects in ever-changing and complex environments. Additionally, CapsNets can be used to detect relationships between objects in a scene, whereas traditional deep learning networks are limited to identifying individual objects.

36 List out the disadvantages of capsule neural network

ANSWER Capsule neural networks have several disadvantages that should be taken into consideration when deciding whether or not to use them.

- The complexity makes them difficult to train, as they require a large amount of data to accurately predict outcomes. In addition, the complexity also makes them prone to errors in prediction and can result in more errors than other approaches. Furthermore, they may require more computing power and may not be suitable for certain applications with limited resources.
- Capsule neural networks are not as well understood as other approaches, such as recurrent or convolutional neural networks. This means there is less knowledge available on how to configure a capsule neural network for a given task and how to tune the parameters for better performance.

- Capsule neural networks are still a relatively new approach, so there are not as many resources available and it can be difficult to find pre-trained models that have been tested and proven to be effective. This can be problematic if the goal is to quickly build a working system.

37 Explain Maximum Likelihood Estimation

ANSWER Maximum Likelihood Estimation (MLE) is a statistical method used to estimate the parameters of a probability distribution by maximizing the likelihood function. It is widely used in various fields, including statistics, econometrics, machine learning, and data science.

MLE consists of the following components:

Likelihood function: The likelihood function measures the probability of observing the given data as a function of the unknown parameters. It is denoted by $L(\theta \mid x)$, where θ represents the parameters of the distribution and x represents the observed data. The likelihood function essentially quantifies how likely the observed data is under a particular set of parameter values.

Parameter estimation: The goal of MLE is to find the values of the parameters θ that maximize the likelihood function. In other words, it seeks the parameter values that make the observed data most probable. Mathematically, we express this as:

$$\hat{\theta} = \text{argmax } L(\theta \mid x)$$

The $\hat{\theta}$ represents the estimated values of the parameters that maximize the likelihood function.

Optimization: Finding the maximum likelihood estimates involves optimization techniques. This typically requires taking the derivative of the likelihood function with respect to the parameters and setting it equal to zero to find the maximum. Depending on the complexity of the problem, analytical solutions may not always be available, and numerical optimization algorithms, such as gradient descent or Newton's method, are used.

MLE has several desirable properties, including consistency, efficiency, and asymptotic normality. Consistency means that as the sample size increases, the MLE converges to the true parameter values. Efficiency implies that the MLE achieves the lowest possible variance among all consistent estimators. Asymptotic normality means that as the sample size grows larger, the MLE follows a normal distribution with a mean centered at the true parameter values.

38 Define loss and loss Function for training Machine Learning Models

ANSWER

In the context of machine learning, loss refers to a measure of how well a machine learning model's prediction align with the true values or labels in the training data. It quantifies the discrepancy or error between the predicted outputs and the actual outputs. The goal of training a machine learning model is to minimize this loss.

A loss function, also known as an objective function or cost function, is a mathematical function that calculates the loss or error of the model's predictions. It takes the predicted output and the true output as inputs and produces a single scalar value that represents the model's performance on the training data.

The choice of the loss function depends on the specific machine learning task at hand. Different tasks, such as regression, classification, or sequence generation, may require different loss functions. Here are a few common loss functions:

Mean Squared Error (MSE): It is used for regression tasks, MSE measures the average squared difference between the predicted and true values. It is defined as:

$$MSE = (1/n) * \Sigma(y - ŷ)^2$$

where

y = represents the true values

ŷ = represents the predicted values

n = is the number of samples.

Binary Cross-Entropy Loss: It is used for binary classification problems, this loss function quantifies the dissimilarity between the predicted probabilities and the true binary labels. It is given by:

$$BCE = -(y * \log(ŷ) + (1 - y) * \log(1 - ŷ))$$

where

y = is the true label (0 or 1)

ŷ = is the predicted probability of the positive class.

Categorical Cross-Entropy Loss: This is suitable for multi-class classification problems; this loss function measures the dissimilarity between the predicted class probabilities and the true class labels. It is expressed as:

$$CCE = -\Sigma(y * \log(ŷ))$$

where

y = is a one-hot encoded vector representing the true class label

ŷ = is the predicted probability distribution over the classes.

Hinge Loss: This is commonly used for support vector machines (SVMs) and binary classification tasks, hinge loss penalizes misclassifications and encourages correct predictions with a margin. It is defined as:

Hinge Loss = max(0, 1 - y * ŷ)

where

y = is the true label (either -1 or 1)

ŷ = is the predicted output.

These are many other loss functions depending on the specific requirements of the machine learning problem. The choice of the loss function influences the learning behavior of the model during training, and finding an appropriate loss function is crucial for achieving desired results.

39. Define Federated Learning.

ANSWER Federated learning is a machine learning approach that enables model training across multiple decentralized devices or servers without exchanging raw data. In federated learning, the training data remains distributed across edge devices, such as smartphones, IoT devices, or servers, and model updates are computed locally on each device. These local updates are then aggregated to create a global model, which is iteratively refined through collaboration among the devices.

40 List out the key characteristics of Federated Learning.

ANSWER The key characteristics of Federated Learning are as follows:

- **Privacy Preservation:** Federated learning enables model training while keeping the training data decentralized and local to each device. This helps preserve user privacy by avoiding the need to share sensitive data with a central server.
- **Decentralized Training:** In federated learning, model training is performed locally on each device using its local data. This decentralized approach allows training to occur in environments where data cannot be easily centralized, such as mobile devices or edge computing systems.
- **Collaborative Learning:** Federated learning involves collaboration among devices to collectively improve the global model. Local model updates are aggregated and combined to generate a more accurate and robust global model that reflects the collective knowledge of all devices.
- **Reduced Communication Costs:** By performing model updates locally and aggregating them centrally, federated learning reduces the need for communication between devices and central servers. This helps minimize bandwidth usage and latency, making federated learning suitable for resource-constrained environments.
- **Adaptability to Heterogeneous Data:** Federated learning can accommodate heterogeneous data distributions across devices or servers. Each device can train its local model using its unique data distribution, and the global model can adapt to diverse data sources by aggregating local updates.

41 List out the challenges that needs to be addressed in federated learning.

ANSWER Federated learning presents several challenges that need to be addressed to ensure its successful implementation and deployment in various applications. Some of the key challenges include:

- **Communication Efficiency:** Federated learning requires frequent communication between edge devices and the central server for model updates and aggregation. Communication overhead can be significant, especially in networks with limited bandwidth or high latency. Efficient communication protocols and strategies are needed to minimize communication costs and ensure timely model updates.

- **Model Aggregation:** Aggregating local model updates from a large number of devices while preserving model accuracy and convergence poses a challenge. Federated averaging, the most common aggregation method, may suffer from issues such as non-IID data distributions, device heterogeneity, and outlier detection. Developing robust aggregation algorithms that account for these factors is essential for maintaining model quality.

- **Privacy and Security:** Federated learning aims to preserve user privacy by keeping data decentralized and local to devices. Threats such as model inversion attacks, membership inference attacks, and data poisoning attacks need to be addressed through privacy-preserving techniques such as differential privacy, secure aggregation, and cryptographic protocols.

- **Data Heterogeneity and Non-IID Data:** Edge devices in federated learning environments may have diverse data distributions and characteristics, leading to challenges related to non-IID (non-independent and identically distributed) data. Model performance can be negatively affected if the local data distributions differ significantly from the global distribution. Techniques for handling data heterogeneity, such as adaptive aggregation methods and data augmentation strategies, are necessary to mitigate this challenge.
- **Resource Constraints:** Edge devices in federated learning environments, such as smartphones, IoT devices, and edge servers, often have limited computational resources, memory, and energy. Training complex models on resource-constrained devices can be challenging and may require model compression techniques, lightweight architectures, and efficient training algorithms to ensure feasibility and scalability.
- **Fairness and Bias:** Federated learning models may inherit biases present in the local data distributions, leading to unfair or biased predictions. Ensuring fairness and mitigating bias in federated learning systems is crucial for promoting ethical AI and preventing discriminatory outcomes. Techniques for bias detection, bias mitigation, and fairness-aware training need to be integrated into federated learning pipelines.

- **Model Robustness and Generalization:** Federated learning models may be vulnerable to adversarial attacks, distribution shifts, and other sources of model degradation. Robustness techniques, such as adversarial training, data augmentation, and regularization, are needed to enhance model resilience and generalization across diverse environments.

42 Explain the working of Federated Learning.

ANSWER The working of federated learning involves several steps that enable model training across multiple decentralized devices or servers while preserving data privacy. Here's an overview of the typical workflow of federated learning as shown in figure 11.10.

Step 1: Initialization: The process begins with the initialization of a global model by the central server or orchestrator. This global model serves as the starting point for training and will be iteratively refined through collaboration with decentralized devices.

Step 2: Device Selection: The central server selects a subset of decentralized devices, such as smartphones, IoT devices, or edge servers, to participate in the federated learning process. The selection criteria may depend on factors such as device availability, connectivity, and resource constraints.

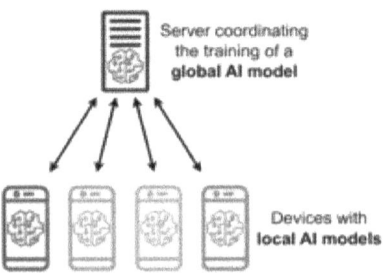

Figure 11.10: Workflow of Federated Learning

Step 3: Model Distribution: The global model is distributed to the selected devices, where it is deployed locally for training. Each device trains the model using its local data without sharing raw data or sensitive information with the central server or other devices.

Step 4: Local Training: On each device, the local model is trained using locally available data. The training process involves computing gradients based on the device's data and updating the model parameters to minimize a loss function, typically using stochastic gradient descent (SGD) or a variant.

Step 5: Model Update: After local training, each device generates a model update consisting of the changes to the model parameters. These updates are computed based on the local gradients and represent the device's local knowledge or insights learned from its data.

Step 6: Secure Aggregation: The model updates from all participating devices are securely aggregated by the central server to compute a global model update. Secure aggregation techniques, such as secure multi-party computation (MPC) or cryptographic protocols, are used to protect the privacy of individual updates during aggregation.

Step 7: Model Integration: The aggregated global model update is integrated into the global model by the central server. This update reflects the collective knowledge and insights learned from all participating devices and is used to refine the global model for the next iteration.

Step 8: Iterative Refinement: Steps 3 to 7 are repeated iteratively for multiple rounds or epochs. In each round, a new subset of devices is selected, and the process of model distribution, local training, model update, secure aggregation, and model integration is performed to further refine the global model.

Step 9: Convergence: The federated learning process continues until the global model converges to a satisfactory level of performance or stability. Convergence criteria may include reaching a predefined accuracy threshold, achieving consistency across devices, or completing a fixed number of iterations.

Step 10: Deployment: Once the global model has converged, it can be deployed for inference or further evaluation in real-world applications. The final model represents a collaborative effort among decentralized devices, with contributions from diverse data sources while preserving user privacy and data confidentiality.

BIBLIOGRAPHY

1. https://pytorch.org/
2. https://www.tensorflow.org/
3. https://scikit-learn.org/
4. https://xgboost.readthedocs.io
5. https://keras.io/
6. https://www.statsmodels.org/
7. https://scipy.org/
8. https://numpy.org/
9. https://www.python.org/

INDEX

A

Accuracy 90
Activation function 151
Activation function layer 165
Alternate Hypothesis 41
A/B Testing 69
Artificial intelligence 162
Artificial neural network 148
Autoencoder 173
Average pooling 166

B

Backpropagation 158
Bagging 91, 180
Bayesian Inference 70
Baye's theorem 60
Bernoulli classifier 112
Bias 94
Binary logistic regression 120
Binary step function 151
Binomial distribution 55
Boltzmann machine 178
Bottleneck 174
Boosting 91, 180

Box plots 23

C

Categorical Data 1
CART algorithm 134, 136
Capsule neural network 190
Causation 46
Central Tendency 7,38
Central Limit theorem 45
Chance nodes 135
Classification 83,88, 115
Cluster Analysis 24
Clustering 84
Cluster Sampling 27
Confidence Interval 67
Confusion matrix 88
Conditional Probability 58
Continuous Data 2,4
Continuous Probability Distribution 53,54
Convolutional autoencoders 175
Convolutional neural network 164,165
Convenience Sampling 28

Correlation 10,11, 47
Cosine similarity 102
Cost function 154
Covariance 10,11
Cross validation 95
Curse of dimensionality 105

D

Data 1,
Data analytics 99
Data dredging 68
Data leakage 95
Dataset 5
Data science 97
Data Visualization 4
Decision nodes 135
Decision tree 130
Decoder 174
Deep learning 162, 172
Dependence 58
Descriptive analysis 98
Diagnostic analysis 98
Dimensionality reduction 84,91
Discrete Data 2,3
Discrete Probability distribution 54
Dispersion 39
Distribution 6
Dropout 161

E

Empirical rule 63

End nodes 135
Ensemble learning 91
Entropy 134
Expected value 52
Exploratory Data Analysis 9
Exponential function 117
Exponential Linear Unit function 152
Evaluation 188

F

F1 score 90
False negative 89
False positive 89
Feature scaling 137
Federated learning 194
Feed forward network 155, 179
Filters 166
Fine-tuning 187
Fourier transform 171
Freezing layers 187
Fully connected layer 166, 170

G

Gain ratio 133
Gaussian mixture model 106
Generalized discriminant analysis 93
Gini impurity 136
Gini index 133
Global minima 77

Gradient descent 72

H

hidden layer 148
Hyperparameters 160, 180
Hypothesis 40
Hypothesis Testing 40

I

ID3 algorithm 133, 136
Independence 58
Inductive bias 141
Inductive transfer learning 184, 186
Information gain 133

J

Jaccard similarity 102

K

k-fold cross validation 96
k-means 106, 108
k-means clustering 106,108
k-nearest neighbor 100, 103
k-nn imputer 104
Kurtosis 32

L

L1 regularization 127
L2 regularization 128
Laplacian filter 167

Lasso regression 124
Leptokurtic 32
Leaky ReLU function 152
Likelihood 48
Linear discriminant analysis 92
Linear function 116, 152
Linear regression 118, 147
Local minima 77
Local Outlier Factor 23
Logarithmic function 114
Logistic regression 120
Lossless encoding 172
Lossy encoding 172
LSTM 177

M

Machine learning 78, 162
Mahalanobis distance 23
Manhattan distance 102
Max pooling 166
Maximum likelihood estimation 191
Mean 38
Measurement Scales 8
Median 20,38
Mesokurtic 32
Minkowski distance 102
Mode 38
Model 78
Multicollinearity 117
Multi-layer perceptron model 156

Multinomial classifier 112
Multinomial logistic regression 121
Multiple linear regression 118

N

Naïve baye's classifer 110
Naïve baye's 111
Negative Skew 30
Neural network 148
Neurons 148, 153
Nominal Data 2
Normal Distribution 18
Null HypothesSis 41
Numerical Data 1,6

O

One-tailed test 66
Ordinal Data 2,3,6
Ordinal logistic regression 121
Optimization 192
Optimizers 160
Outliers 21,22
Overfitting 80
Overfitting trees 132

P

Parameterized ReLU function 152
Pareto Principle 33
p-hacking 68
perceptron 150,153
Platykurtic 32

Poisson distribution 57
Pool layer 165
Polynomial function 116
Population 5
Positive Skew 30
Power function 117
Precision 90
Prescriptive analysis 98
Principal component analysis 92
Probability 48, 52
Probability Density Function 13,15
Probability Distribution 53
Probability Mass Function 15
Probability Sampling 26
Pruning 144
P – values 44

Q

Qualitative Data 1
Quantitative Data 1
Quota Sampling 28

R

Random Variable 51
Recall 89
Regression 83, 114
Regularization 127,160
Reinforced learning 84
ReLU function 152
Residual 72
Residual sum of squares 72

Ridge regression 125
RNN 176, 179
Root Cause Analysis 37

S

Sample 5
Sampling 24
Self-transfer learning 185
Semi-supervised transfer learning 185
Sensitivity 89
Sequential transfer learning 184
Sigmoid function 121, 152
Similarity 101
Simple Random Sampling 27
Simpson's Paradox 43
Simple linear regression 118
Single layer perceptron model 155
Skewness 30
Snowball Sampling 28
Softmax function 153
Specificity 89
Splitting nodes 132
Standard Deviation 15
Stacking 91
Stratified Sampling 27
Step size 74
Stochastic gradient descent 75
Supervised learning 82, 85, 87
Swish function 153
Systematic Sampling 27

T

Tanh function 152
Transductive transfer learning 184, 186
Transfer learning 181
True negative 89
True positive 89
True negative rate 89
True positive rate 89
Turkey's Method 23
Type I Error 41
Type II Error 42
Two-tailed test 65

U

Underfitting 80
Unsupervised learning 83, 86, 87
Unsupervised transfer learning 185

V

Variable 1,
Variability 8,
Variance 12, 94
Variational autoencoder 176

W

Weight 150
Weight update 159

X

Y

Z

Z-Scores 23
Z-values 48

ABOUT THE FRONT COVER PAGE DESIGN

*T*he dancer on the front cover page depicts the dance form of Kuchipudi, capturing the essence of Kuchipudi in its entirety. The dancer is dancing blissfully to the sublime divine blessings of Lord Krishna himself.

Kuchipudi is considered one of the eight major Indian classical dances. Kuchipudi dance form has its origin in a small village called Kuchipudi (also called Kuchelapuram) of Krishna district of Andhra Pradesh, India, in the 7th century. Kuchipudi is an expressive dance form that connects and depicts the stories of Lord Krishna through gestures and facial expressions.

The front cover page design was adapted from the artwork of Mr. Bijay Biswaal (@BijayBiswaal on X social media platform) who was gracious enough to permit us to use it.

www.ingramcontent.com/pod-product-compliance
Lightning Source LLC
LaVergne TN
LVHW061543070526
838199LV00077B/6886